MW01275612

Against All Terrors

This People's Next Defense

by

Philip Gold

Seattle   Discovery Institute Press   2002

Against All Terrors was written by Philip Gold in the aftermath of the September 11, 2001 terrorist attacks in New York City and Washington, D.C.

Library Cataloging Data

Gold, Philip (1948–)

Against All Terrors: This People's Next Defense

151 p. 23 cm.

ISBN 0-9638654-6-3 (pbk.: alk paper)

LC 2002100698

Keywords: Terrorism, National Defense, Homeland Security, Military Transformation, International Relations

Discovery Institute Press, Seattle, WA

Internet: http://www.Discovery.org/

Published in the United States of America on acid-free paper

First Edition, First Printing, February 2002

"Poll: Americans Starting to Doubt War."

—Associated Press, 30 October 2001

"You cannot conquer America."

—William Pitt in the House of Commons,
18 November 1777

Most often, books are dedicated to people whom the author knows, and who have figured importantly in his life and work. However, I've chosen to dedicate this book to people I may never meet; whose names this nation may never know; and whose accomplishments may never be recorded.

In any struggle, any crisis, the heroes are self-selecting: the men and women who come forward, who already have come forward and who will, not just because the moment demands it, but because their spirit and their virtue permit them no alternative. This book is for them, and especially for those who will persevere when (as it must) the war grows long, the nation's ardor evanesces, and unity gives way to business-as-usual.

Which is to say—insofar as we all possess the capacity for heroism—this book is for all of us.

Contents

Preface

The Greeks had two words for time. One was *chronos*, chronological time, the orderly passing of the intervals by which we measure existence and events. The other word, *kairos*, has no English equivalent. It can mean, variously, the right time, the critical time, the fullness of time. Its connotations are emergency and crisis, but also inevitability and fulfillment. *Kairos* is the moment that had to happen.

On September 11th, 2001, the people of the United States of America entered *kairos*. We're going to be there for a while. The question is, what do we do with the months and years that follow the moment that had to happen? *Against All Terrors* offers one kind of answer.

I work as Senior Fellow in National Security Affairs at Discovery Institute, a Seattle-based think tank. By academic training, I'm an historian of American culture. I've taught defense and cultural history at Georgetown University, and have written extensively on both. When the *kairos* of 9/11 arrived, and after the initial brace of emotions receded a bit, I did what think tank experts and pundits often do. Through our organizations and our media contacts, we make ourselves "available for comment."

I'd done it before, and it had always struck me as a bit ghoulish, this pushing yourself forward because of crisis or catastrophe. And at first it was ghoulish indeed. But within a day or two, I realized that I might be able to provide a useful service. People needed anyone who could help them make sense of the horror and the changes of soul it was already engendering. They wanted some notion of what had to be done, beyond the obvious initial tasks of justice and war. And they were curious about the nation, about us, and about the people we might now have to become.

As the weeks went on, two other things became apparent. The media were defaulting to their usual mode. With their nonstop bombardment of momentous repetition and trivial commentary ("All Anthrax All The Time" and "Airport Security 24/7"), they were leaving us informed to stupefaction, yet knowing practically nothing. The more they talked, the less they said. Even those who supported the government's efforts seemed compelled to offer criticism for criticism's sake, or to cloak their ignorance with vague yet dire warnings of what *might* happen if we failed . . . or if we succeeded. Either something was taking too long or, if they didn't feel that was the proper thing to say, it wasn't going fast enough. Or maybe it was going too fast.

As the media reverted to form, so did the Culture Warriors. It was back to Culture Wars business-as-usual—sniping, preening, gleefully seizing on each other's gaffes, huffing their dudgeon and their pouts. And I found myself wondering:

Is this the best we can do? Is all this really worthy of us?

So I decided to offer something different, a mix of military analysis and cultural suggestion that might get beyond the dueling clichés. I did print. I did panels. I gave speeches. I did radio. I even morphed into a local TV talking head—and learned to my considerable embarrassment that it ain't as easy as it looks. But I did find that providing historical and cultural context, attempting a longer-term view, mattered greatly. I also found that people welcomed complex and non-trivial answers to three questions. What kind of world is this now? What defenses will be required? And are we a people capable of carrying the struggle for as long as it takes?

These are the questions that neither the media nor the experts nor the Culture Warriors have answered. Yes, we can do better than they've done so far. Yes, we must.

Then a sustained period of literary procrastination paid off. Since the mid-nineties, I'd wanted to write a general-audience defense book, a primer on the complexities of twenty-first century defense.[1] In 2000, I'd more or less finished a first draft of *Against All Terrors*, focused on what's known in the trade as "transformation," and on the then-neglected subject of homeland defense.[2] I'd hesitated to publish it or, more honestly, to complete it prior to the 2000 election, not

---

1. This book actually began with a sneer. I'd approached a senior executive of a major defense contractor with a proposal to do a general-audience book. His response came back fast, loud, and clear. "You're wrong. All the American people need to know is, Spend Money." That motivated me.

2. For nearly a decade, Discovery Institute has urged serious homeland defense and predicted the advent of mass terrorism on American soil. Many of the measures Discovery has advocated are now coming to pass. These papers, columns, and articles are available at the Discovery website, www.discovery.org.

AGAINST ALL TERRORS

wanting it to turn into yet another sterile anti-Clinton diatribe and brain-dead demand for promiscuous defense spending. After the Bush administration took office, the manuscript developed into a strong support of Defense Secretary Donald Rumsfeld's attempts to drag the defense establishment into the twenty-first century. We'd planned to bring it out after Mr. Rumsfeld's intentions had become clear, and his opponents were openly arrayed.

In any event, a few days after 9/11, I suggested to my boss that now might be the right time to bring out the book, with three provisos. We had to stick to our plan of writing a short, accessible book. This could not be the standard once-you-put-it-down-you-can't-pick-it-up-again think tank tome. The target audience had to be people who, prior to the attack, would have had little interest in defense affairs, indeed, might not have been caught dead reading about it. And most importantly, the book also had to address the subject of *us*. Nearly two centuries ago, Karl von Clausewitz described war as the endeavor of a "remarkable trinity" of the state, the military, and the people. Without the sustained support and participation of the people, the endeavor could not succeed. His dictum remains valid today, even for—perhaps especially for—a war such as this.

My boss agreed. I set to work. I delivered the manuscript only a few weeks late. Writerly procrastination dies hard. I was also blessed with some excellent outside readers, recruited in some cases for their expertise, in others for their total lack of it. Thanks to John Titcomb, Deborah Berglund, Bob and Marcia Gold, Marianne and Michael McDonald, Nina Shapiro. Thanks also to Lt. Col. Kevin ("Buffman") Cole, USAF, decorated Desert Storm aviator, for many thoughts over many months. Thanks also to a few guys whose day jobs prohibit mention of their names.

Three very special mentions. Retired Marine Major Tony Milavic, a three-tour Vietnam vet (plus other adventures) who now runs MILINET, a magnificent private Internet news service/discussion site for the military and intelligence communities and those who love them. My MILINET e-comrades have been a delightful source of information, expertise, lore, and on-line company. Well-done, Tony. *Semper Fi.* Thanks also to Greg Barlow of the Medina Foundation. Medina has supported my defense work over the years, and came through with a quick post-9/11 grant to help publicize this book. Greg Barlow, a decorated Vietnam Green Beret and retired

Adjutant General of the Washington State National Guard, has also been a major source of military insight and personal inspiration.

Gratitude also to some people—several hundred by now—whom I've never met, but who over the last couple years read my articles, saw or heard my media gigs, and got in touch to share their thoughts. It wasn't always flattering. It occasionally got heated. But it was always stimulating and valuable.

Thanks also to Mike Perry, who worked his customary formatting magic on the text and to Joel Shoop, who did the cover with his usual brilliance and good cheer.

Finally, to the folks at Discovery, I happily acknowledge my debts. Ambassador Bruce Chapman, founding president of the Institute, boss, friend, critic, and Christian gentleman of the old school. Would that we had a few thousand—or a few million—more like him around. The same can be said for Bob Cihak, MD, Discovery board member, friend and mentor, who funded the early work. Special thanks to Tom Alberg, a Discovery board member who, literally hours after 9/11, called Bruce to ask what he could do. Tom funded the rewrite and initial publication costs.

Two other Discovery board members provided additional opportunities. Fred Weiss arranged for me to deliver a speech on these themes to the Seattle Rotary Club; Rotarian feedback proved invaluable. Also, former Congressman John Miller went out of his way to generate media opportunities.

Finally, regards to the rest of Discovery Institute, especially Steve Buri, Doug Bilderback, and Jay Richards, who were actively engaged in this work throughout. Good colleagues, good people, good friends. Within most writers there resides a child with an endless urge to grab his latest little epiphany or accomplishment and go running down the hall, shouting, "Look what I did!" I've done it to them considerably more than once, disturbed their own endeavors considerably more than once, and they've been unfailingly patient, indulgent, and benign. Thanks again.

Seattle, Washington
January 2002

Introduction

Words matter. They matter because meaning, not force, is the essence of civilization. Force only defends it or destroys it.

Our Founding Fathers understood this. The Declaration of Independence held that a "decent respect to the opinions of mankind" required a statement of why they'd chosen to take up arms, and commit thereby the crime of high treason against the most powerful empire on earth. Of course, back then "opinion" didn't carry its present meaning of "Everybody's Entitled and One's as Good as Any Other and Who Are You to Judge?" Nor was opinion merely a matter of number. Opinion meant reasoned judgment, in some ways the human obligation to make reasoned judgment. And reason in the eighteenth century lexicon meant the human ability to apprehend and comprehend reality: that which is. Opinion wasn't quite the same as truth. But it had no room for deliberate falsehood or for deceit, for self-deception or for spin.

But that was then. This is post-then. What words, what meanings, what judgments might matter now?

As I write, the shock of 9/11 has ebbed, although if you believe the media and the surveys, anti-anxiety pills are selling like Lotto tickets and one in four Americans has trouble sleeping. Or is the real news that most Americans aren't popping pills and three out of four can sleep? The prayers have been said, the anthems sung; the flags, at last in plentiful supply (courtesy of all those Chinese factories), seem everywhere. The anti-terrorism legislation has been passed, the ludicrously over-acronymed USA PATRIOT Act: "Uniting and Strengthening America by Providing Appropriate Tools Required to Intercept and Obstruct Terrorism." The first tens of the emergency billions have been appropriated. The annual defense budget now runs over $340 billion, with more to follow. Anthrax has become a fixture of our national life; airline security, yet another obsession. We worry about the next event. And the great grim machinery of war does its work.

As I review these words before going to press, it's mid-January. Four months. Seems like forever, and also only yesterday. *Kairos* is like that. A few weeks ago, no one seemed happy with either the pace of the action or the results . . . as though reality had to conform to media schedules and popular attention spans, and victory is measured by opinion polls, by who and how many feel what. Some took up carping that it was going too slow. On October 30th, conservative columnist Charles Krauthammer despaired that: "The war is not going well. . . . it has been fought with half-measures."[1]

Four weeks later, most of Afghanistan (subject to change without notice) belonged to the Marines and the anti-Taliban, and Dr. Krauthammer was running items headlined "Victory Changes Everything."[2] At the other end of the spectrum of respectable opinion, Frank Rich spent October moaning about ". . . the multitude of ways we're losing the war at home."[3] Then came the raids on alleged terrorist financing facilities and a flurry of law enforcement and National Guard activity, and Mr. Rich and his fellow Olympians of the *New York Times* started complaining that the real problem now was success. We were going too fast. Our victory would plunge Afghanistan into yet another civil war. And our determination to defend ourselves at home would soon submerge civil liberties beneath a perfect storm of government abuse and depredation.

But even as the victories cumulate, the opposition gathers. Some offer words of meaning, spoken in sincerity and good will. Others do not.

There are the principled and absolute pacifists, for whom this new conflict represents only the latest test of commitment. They're worthy of regard, in some cases of personal respect, even though they would surrender the world to evil. Then there are those with nothing to talk about save their feelings and their fears, those who ground their opposition in personal emotion. Sorry, our long national group therapy session is over. And "conscience"—from the Latin, *con sciere*—means literally to "know with" or to "know together." Those with nothing to talk about save themselves offer not conscience, but monologue.

---

1. Charles Krauthammer, "Not Enough Might," *Washington Post,* 30 October 2001, p. A-21.
2. Charles Krauthammer, "Victory Changes Everything," *Washington Post,* 30 November 2001, p. A-41.
3. Frank Rich, "How to Lose a War," *New York Times,* 27 October 2001, Early Bird.

AGAINST ALL TERRORS

There are the principled civil libertarians, for whom this new conflict represents only the latest test of commitment. They're worthy of careful attention, especially given some of the scarier provisos of the new anti-terrorism legislation regarding detention, seizure, and information-gathering and the possible draconian expansion of "emergency public health powers." Still, at issue here is not so much the new powers themselves as how they're used and abused; what oversight must be provided; and how quickly and fairly the innocent are compensated for whatever losses they suffer. The principled libertarians should devote themselves to these matters, rather than to the standard "slippery-slope" prognostications that if we change the present and highly idiosyncratic structure of civil liberties even one iota today, it's concentration camps and Big Brother tomorrow. As *New York Times* columnist Bob Herbert put it, "If human beings are involved, mistakes will be made." And then, in a moment of genuine grace, he added: "And it is not unpatriotic to warn that in a period of tremendous fear and anxiety, public officials might pose a threat to the principles of justice and fairness that have made this nation the jewel of the planet."[4]

Way to go.

Then there are those—an ugly congeries of ideologues—who confuse civil liberties with the freedom to do anything they damn well please, regardless of external realities and common perils. The Greeks had a word for people who concerned themselves only with their private desires and affairs. They called them *Idiotes*. When our children behave thus, we call them spoiled brats. Whatever else may be said of the civil liberties conundrum, dead people cannot exercise their rights. And whatever else may be said of the Constitution, it is not a suicide pact.

There are those who understand that America's actions in the world are rarely pristine or perceived as such. No nation's policies ever are. Yes, we've sometimes supported foreign leaders abhorrent to their own peoples. Often, especially during the Cold War, we had valid reasons for doing so. From time to time, such support spared those peoples even greater horrors, and afforded them the subsequent luxury of despising us for the services rendered. Greece comes to mind. So does Kuwait. So will Afghanistan; let's not expect a whole

---

4. Bob Herbert, "Mistakes Will Be Made," *New York Times,* 10 December 2001, Early Bird.

lot of thanks down the road. Still, those who counsel us to understand how and why so many hate us, and why even our friends often experience an intense discomfort, are important. We have done harm in this world, and in many ways need to change our policies and improve our behavior.

Then there are those who want us paralyzed by guilt and shame, who would use our history to manipulate, control, and defeat us. But as the saying goes, "When the Devil tells you about your past, tell the Devil about your future."[5] While you're at it, ask him who the hell he is to be accusing anybody of anything. And anyway, most of the rest of the world doesn't exactly seem to be celebrating diversity these days.

Then there's the old "America: Just Hate It" crowd, so dreary, weary, and eminently predictable. Let Susan Sontag (who once called the white race the "cancer of humanity"), writing in the *New Yorker*, stand in: "The disconnect between last Tuesday's monstrous dose of reality and the self-righteous drivel and outright deceptions being peddled by public figures and TV commentators is startling. The voices licensed to follow the event seem to have joined together in a campaign to infantilize the public."[6] For those wishing to peruse other examples, especially the utterances of the "Blame America First" crowd, the American Council of Trustees and Alumni has published a compendium of self-flagellation.[7] We pass over in silence the silence of so many "stars" in and of the entertainment business, save to note that their agents and their employers seem to have told them to shut up for a while if they want to keep on working.

Of course, not everyone sees it this way. Aaron Sorkin, creator of the popular TV series "West Wing," charges that it's McCarthy Black List all over again. "What is important," he says, "is dissent."[8] Not support. Not participation. Dissent. Whence comes this notion that

---

5. My colleague Jay Richards, who holds a Ph.D. from Princeton Theological Seminary, tells me that the proper quote is, "When the Devil tells you about your past, ask the Devil about his future."

6. Quoted in Brink Lindsey, "Terrorism's Fellow Travelers," *Cato Policy Report,* Nov./Dec. 2001, p. 11.

7. American Council of Trustees and Alumni, "Defending Civilization: How Our Universities Are Failing America and What Can be Done about It," available for free download at www.goacta.org.

8. "Sorkin Charges: 'Blacklist' Is 'Happening All Over Again,'" *Drudge Report,* 26 Oct. 2001, Internet.

protest is always and forever a superior form of morality, or the belief that just because speech is free, it should always and forever also be without consequences? America protects expression. America does not guarantee respect, and is not obliged to provide or subsidize platforms, or to stifle disagreement with dissent.

Then there are those who warn us what a long, difficult, and costly struggle lies ahead. Despite the wondrous victories of the autumn of 2001, they're correct. We do well to heed them, and especially well to remember that "it ain't over 'til it's over," in Afghanistan or wherever terrorism metastasizes. But there are also those who take counsel of their fears, sometimes to the point of seeming to wish for national paralysis of will. There's the "What About?" crowd, rummaging through history—Vietnam, the Soviets or British in Afghanistan, the Crusades—to "prove" that we must fail because others have. Their analogies didn't prevent the Taliban from collapsing. Then there are those who invoke the "desire for martyrdom" as some sort of all-purpose dissuasion. General Patton, loosely paraphrased and sanitized, answered them best. No one ever won a war by dying for his country (or movement). He won by making some one else die.

And then there are those who warn of Islamic "backlash" or "fragile coalitions" as insurmountable obstacles. If nothing else, the Afghan campaign demonstrated that Islamic "backlash" is inversely proportional to the efficacy of American arms. Power also talks. As for fragile coalitions—such is the nature of nearly all such arrangements. Then there are those who oppose almost anything on the grounds that somebody somewhere might not like it. "The world community," perhaps. "The court of world opinion," most definitely. Were it not for the facts that there is no world community, only a tiny, sadly strife-torn globe, and that "world opinion" can neither be measured nor enforced, they'd have a point.

Yes, in the end everything human falls short. Few victories are ever final or complete. Today's successes generate tomorrow's problems. Decisions correct in the short run may turn into long-term mistakes. All this is true. Nonetheless, some people seem to have nothing to offer but fear itself.

Then there are those who warn that, in fighting our enemies, we must not sink to their level. They have a point. Certain actions, such as indiscriminate terror attacks on civilians, are and will be neither morally justified nor militarily useful. In fact, we've been getting out of that business for ages. The lavish use of brute firepower that used to characterize the "American Way of War" is ending. Over the last several decades, we have spent trillions of dollars—*trillions*—making our weaponry less destructive and more precise. Almost weekly, it seems, Defense Secretary Donald Rumsfeld and a phalanx of senior officers apologize for the death and injury of civilians, many of whom were unlawfully endangered by the enemy, which embeds its military forces and facilities among them. It's common practice in Iraq, also. We're going to see it again.

But there are also those who demand that we maintain such a level of purity, so hedge ourselves about with restrictions and legalisms and "rules of engagement" that effective action becomes impossible. In truth, a morality that demands impossible levels of purity has less to do with morality than with insanity, or at best with a Pharisaical perversion of morality. And never—*never*—has there been a nation at war more solicitous of the welfare of innocents than America today. Historically, conquerors and empires have relied on terror to compensate for weakness. Some left pyramids of skulls. Others left roads lined with crosses, made examples of cities, annihilated peoples. Their purpose was to intimidate and deter. Today, we also seek to intimidate and deter. But how differently we do it. Perhaps Operation Enduring Freedom has two great symbols: precision-guided weaponry and air-dropped "culturally sensitive" emergency rations.

Something else might be said here. It's not often said because we are not a people who enjoys saying it. But perhaps the world needs to hear it. The only thing standing between America's enemies and annihilation is American restraint. Six nukes and Afghanistan would have been back in the Pleistocene. Somalia, Ethiopia, Sudan, the same. Twenty nukes would dispatch Iraq to the far side of the Neolithic. But we don't. Nor will we. War is Hell, said General Sherman, and you cannot refine it. But there are degrees of Hell. Wanton, indiscriminate brutality is not our twenty-first century way, nor any longer a necessary means of war.

Finally—and for our purposes, most importantly—there are those who understand the reality of the situation, the extent of the peril, and the necessity of prolonged and effective action. But they're also uneasy; they acknowledge a certain bewilderment. They know intuitively that Mr. Rumsfeld was right when he said at a September news conference: "We really, almost, are going to have to fashion a new vocabulary and different constructs for thinking about what it is that we're doing."[9] New words, new concepts . . . and perhaps also some very old concepts, rediscovered and renewed to fit the times.

But what concepts avail us now? What words for the people we have become after the Culture War of the last forty years? Nations fight or fail to fight with what they have, spiritually and intellectually and culturally as well as militarily. If it is true that there has never been a war such as this, it is also true that there has never been a people such as us to fight it.

So what truths, what principles now?

Against All Terrors suggests one possible answer. It does so by sketching the nature of the age now upon us as well as what kinds of forces will be required. And it suggests that yes, this nation can muster the civic virtue to endure and to prevail.

Against All Terrors comprises four chapters, each with a clarifying theme.

1. The Wars of the Ways

Chapter One, "The Wars of the Ways," offers a style of looking at the new world reality, a style that might be called a paradigm. It may turn out to be a provisional paradigm, but at least it has the virtue of getting beyond the present goulash of trivia and repetition.

The Age of the Wars of Ideology is over. The Age of the Wars of the Ways has begun.

The Wars of the Ways—a protracted global struggle that will pit those who embrace the twenty-first century, its freedoms and potentials, against those who want out or who can't get in. The Wars of the Ways will be fought between those reaching for the stars and those who, to borrow from Milton, would rather reign in Hell than serve in Heaven. Sadly, they will also be fought between those who live amid ever-increasing opulence and those who're barely able to survive. Tragically, and despite our best humanitarian and economic efforts, some among the poorest peoples will lash out in desperation. When you've got nothing, so the old adage goes, you've got nothing to lose.

And sometimes—witness millionaire bin Laden and his impoverished admirers—our two enemies will ally. Sometimes they'll be

9. Secretary of Defense Donald Rumsfeld, "Transcript of Pentagon Press Briefing," 20 Sept. 2001, at www.defenselink.mil.

states. Sometimes they'll be subnational or transnational groups. Sometimes their ostensible reasons will be religious or ethnic, sometimes economic or ecological, sometimes the fruit of philosophies yet to be expounded. Sometimes they'll strike out in hatred, pure and simple. Whatever their motivations, the potential carnage will be horrific, as they increasingly dispose of Weapons of Mass Destruction, or as they've come to be known, WMD.[10]

It is a struggle we dare not lose. When former President Clinton, in a November, 2001 speech at Georgetown University, called the present conflict a "war for the soul of the twenty-first century," he was not wrong.[11] But it's also a war for the soul, perhaps for the very existence of humanity. And in this war, there are certain things that only the United States, by virtue of its military power, can do.

But what is the condition of that power? And what must be done to assure and enhance it?

2. The Wasted Nineties

Chapter Two, "The Wasted Nineties"—a phrase that may someday become as generally accepted and dismissive as "Roaring Twenties" or "Me Decade"—looks to the state of America's defenses as we enter this first of the Wars of the Ways. Yes, Bill Clinton trashed the military. And yes, far too many careerist officers went along. But much of what happened to the military during that decade would have happened under any president. For the deepest problems are systemic.

In essence, this nation's military establishment is an Industrial Age creation, ill-suited to the twenty-first century in general and abysmally prepared for its new missions.

---

10. The term Weapons of Mass Destruction (WMD) is now as much a part of the American lexicon as *Jihad*. Strictly speaking, only nuclear and enhanced conventional explosives are weapons of mass destruction. Biological and chemical weapons are weapons of mass death that attack people, not things. Weapons of mass disruption involve cyberwar or, as the Pentagon prefers to call it, "information operations." Recently, the Pentagon contrived a new acronym, CBRNE: Chemical, Biological, Radiological, Nuclear, Enhanced Conventional Explosive. We'll stick with WMD because it's better known, even if less accurate.

11. Office of Protocol and Events, Georgetown University, "Remarks as Delivered by President William Jefferson Clinton, Georgetown University, November 7th, 2001," at www.georgetown.edu.

The Afghan campaign witnessed this military adapting well, often brilliantly, to the new realities. But adaptation is not reform, and improvisation can only take you so far, and the Afghan campaign may prove more a curiosity than a template for future conflict. The United States is about to pour trillions of dollars into this system— well over a trillion before the 2004 election. A lot of it will be necessary. But much may also be wasted, unless business-as-usual gives way to a disciplined urgency that includes some urgently needed changes.

Fortunately, the Wasted Nineties were not entirely wasted. There is a process known in the trade as "transformation"—rethinking, restructuring, and renewing every aspect of the military. Some have suggested that 9/11 put transformation on indefinite hold. In truth, the reverse is happening, and must happen faster, ever faster. For sooner or later, the entire array of American power will be needed to conduct the Wars of the Ways. It's prudent to assume, sooner rather than later.

3. This People's Next Defense

Chapter Three, "This People's Next Defense," gets into the details of what an effective twenty-first century force might look like. Happily, many of the right things are already under way. But they must be accelerated and brought to fruition. In all cases, a number of enduring principles apply. We begin with these four.

- *Homeland defense comes first.*

- *Aerospace supremacy must be maintained, and the development of space power rapidly expanded.*

- *Conventional forces must develop unsurpassed lethality, flexibility, and mobility—and must be structured for new kinds of technological inter-operability and operational co-operation.*

- *And the American people must re-engage with the common defense.* [12]

In order to realize these principles, a new paradigm, a new way of conceiving defense is necessary. We'll call it "Space Force, Peace Force, Warriors, Guard." It doesn't supersede the present "Army,

---

12. Throughout the book, certain principles and axioms will appear in italicized bold-face. They're collected in the Appendix as "General Principles of Defense Transformation"—an eclectic list and far from exhaustive, but a necessary minimum.

Navy, Air Force, Marines" structure. But it does propose a new way of thinking about who does what, and the transformation challenges each service faces.

None of these changes will happen automatically or easily. Already, resistance is building within The Building, as the Pentagon is sometimes known. Transformation still threatens vested interests. The Defense Department has little love for the homeland security mission, in some case rightly. Inter-service rivalries and budgetary constraints remain. There will never be enough money for everything. It is entirely possible that the defense establishment will fail to adapt, unless the American people engage this issue and let their elected representatives know it.

4. Against All Terrors

The final chapter, "Against All Terrors," considers the character of the American people. In the days after 9/11, Americans came together in a unity of grief not known since John Kennedy's assassination or (for those too young to remember) the Challenger disaster. We came together in a unity of spirit that made three hundred million of us "the smallest town on earth." Genuine patriotism cascaded. So did the wondrous spontaneous humanity that comes in moments of emergency when the trivia falls away and we're free to be our better selves.

But now comes the work of waging this first of the Wars of the Ways. It won't be easy, despite all the recent successes. What inner resources might help us sustain and cohere, perhaps even guide us in the world?

The answer isn't obvious. While everyone may be exposed to a certain statistical degree of danger, and nearly all of us affected economically, only a small percentage of us will be professionally involved. There will be no twentieth century-style total mobilization. Nor will there be a replay of the actions and pressures against the "hyphenated-Americans" of previous wars.[13] Since 9/11, the politicians and the pundits have spoken vigorously against such tawdry recidivism; the prayer services and memorials have worked to include all faiths, all races, all ethnicities. We are, we're told, united in our diversity. And an astonishing respect for diversity it is. No nation in history, under attack and preparing for extended war, has ever—

ever—worried so much about offending people, or about protecting the rights (real and imagined) of those intent upon killing us.

Perhaps such unity-in-diversity will last. But the greater problem remains. Winning a war is not just a matter of unity. It is a matter of effectiveness over time, and the relevant time frame here is years and decades, not weeks and months. How do you and I participate effectively in a complex, conflicted civilization that must provide the effective center of a global struggle against twenty-first century darkness while simultaneously bringing forth the miracles of the twenty-first century, including perhaps a cultural renaissance to match the technological brilliance? What virtues, civic and private, will be needed, as individuals and as a nation? How must they be prudentially applied? As a people, what is worthy of us now?

Can we be good enough? And if so, for how long?

The Founding Fathers show the way. For not only is national defense once again exactly what they envisioned it to be—a continuum of activities—but their conception of the civic virtue of the citizenry is once again relevant.

Or to put it another way, ***twenty-first century perils and technologies bring new vitality to eighteenth century virtues***. Such virtues must be recovered and adapted to the challenges at hand, in a fitting and effective manner. It's not enough to wave the flag, sing "God Bless America," then go about our business. We must make ourselves both strong enough to wage these wars and worthy enough to wage them.

Twice in the twentieth century, the United States saved the planet: once from fascist imperialism, once from Marxist totalitarianism. The current perils may be more diffuse, but are just as real. So are the consequences of failure. Is it arrogant to speak thus? Many would say so. Many would call it an imperial arrogance. Perhaps in some ways it is. But it is also necessary, for the twenty-first century needs guardians. This guardianship, this stewardship of the planet, must take many forms. We'll not be the only guardians. Far from it,

---

13. America's earlier bouts with "war hysteria" go beyond the scope of this book. Suffice it to say, careful study of the "hysterias" of World War I and the Japanese internment of World War II reveals less hysteria than well-planned attacks on certain groups by others. Often, these were the continuation of prewar tensions and rivalries by other means. State and federal governments and politicians acquiesced for reasons of their own. And anyway, you never hear about the hysterias and atrocities and violations that don't happen.

and we must learn to do a far better job of heeding the concerns of others. We hold no monopoly on wisdom. But militarily, we'll be the most important. Yes, we must learn when not to act, and when to let others be strong. But there will be victories that only we can win.

If history shows anything, it's that nothing human is ever automatic or guaranteed. Freedom, prosperity, potential: All can be lost. Some might say that our twentieth century victories were inevitable. Perhaps they were—inevitable to everybody except the men and women who had to go win them. Certainly, neither Act of Congress nor Supreme Court decision nor Executive Order ever decreed America immortal.

Nor is the survival of our species automatic. We are living creatures on a living planet. All that lives can die. And if you believe that this species can destroy itself, and that there is such a thing as ecocide, the murder of the Earth's ability to sustain and nurture life, then here on this our little bit of God's ever-expanding universe, we are the guardians of forever.

1

The Wars of
the Ways

The Age of Wars of Ideology is over. The Age of Wars of the Ways has begun.

The Wars of Ideology. What began at Lexington and Concord in 1775 and Philadelphia a year later; what spread to France and later to much of nineteenth century Europe; what exploded into the great twentieth century struggles against Axis and Marxist totalitarianism, is over. It ended at the Berlin Wall in 1989 and in Moscow's Red Square two years later. And we know now what that era did and meant.

The Wars of Ideology were about great collective issues. What are the proper forms of political and economic organization for nation-states and the societies they govern? From the rational Western perspective at least, those issues have been settled. Liberal democracy and market economy produce and provide more real goods—prosperity, liberty, opportunity—than any alternative yet devised. Freedom works.

When communism fell, it wasn't that hard to imagine a future devoted to the global expansion of liberal democracy and market economy, and the corresponding betterment of the human condition everywhere. Many did.[1] With the Soviets gone and China changing, the twenty-first century would be an era of unsurpassed accomplishment for all. Unsurpassed and unendangered. And for much of the nineties, few Americans thought gloomy. We were prosperous. The world was progressing. Progress—that quintessentially Enlightenment belief that material improvement would also generate peace and moral improvement—seemed, after a couple nasty centuries to be kicking in at last. And Osama bin Laden was somewhere in Afghanistan or the Sudan (who cared?), hanging with the homies and wondering what he might do to re-establish an Islamic empire that hadn't existed for a thousand years. Except this time without that empire's brilliance and tolerance.

We now know what he chose to do. Less commonly understood is the fact that he and his murderous brand of *Jihad* are only Act I, Scene 1 of the Wars of the Ways, a protracted global struggle that will pit those who embrace the twenty-first century against those who

---

1. For a classic statement of this viewpoint, see Francis Fukuyama, "The End of History?" *The National Interest* (Summer 1989), pp. 3–18. See also Francis Fukuyama, *The End of History and the Last Man* (New York: Free Press, 1992).

want out or who can't get in, and who will often find themselves in alliance.

Many want out, for many reasons. Many have declared *Jihad* on the twenty-first century. Violent expansionist Islamic fundamentalists. Ethnic separatists. Eco-terrorists. Anti-globalization fanatics. An endless array of individual and small-group neurotics, psychotics, and malcontents: Unabombers, Timothy McVeighs, perhaps (it may turn out) some domestic jerk with access to anthrax and a penchant for envelope-stuffing. Those who want out, who may also want the world out, and who are prepared to use terror, up to and including genocide and ecocide—these are the *Jehadi* of the twenty-first century. The word may be Arabic in its etymology. But it's common English now.

Then there are others, billions of others, who can't get in. Humanity as a species has reached a critical divide. In the twenty-first century, the difference between rich and poor is no longer a matter of more versus less. Neither is technology merely an issue of access. Humanity—it sounds like science fiction, but it's happening—is on the verge of fissioning into two virtual species. One embraces the twenty-first century, creates, and is formed by the new technologies and the freedoms and possibilities they offer. The other remains in the dust and the mud. One segment of humanity lives aboard space stations, maps the genome, creates fabulous wealth, makes the miraculous routine and the unimaginable trite. The other segment can't get past famine, pestilence, pandemic violence, despair. And the gap is increasing, perhaps exponentially. *New York Times* foreign affairs columnist Tom Friedman tells of a conversation he once had with a Syrian. Those damn Israelis, the man muttered. They've been here fifty years and we're a hundred years behind. Twenty years from now, if the present situation endures, they may well be two centuries behind.

This, then, is the fission. Yes, we can put a PC in every hovel, a cell phone in every hut. We can strew the world with shoe factories. We can feed and vaccinate and contracept and sterilize and abort. But we cannot change people's ways; we cannot mold or manipulate or decree or bomb them into habits and freedoms that work in the twenty-first century. Those changes they must make for themselves. Now, the West holds no monopoly on the human qualities of intelligence, enterprise, diligence. But the West has learned better than anyone else how to liberate more of those qualities for more people. We can show them how to liberate those qualities, how to build markets and cultures and nations. We can educate, aid, and trade. We can, as the old (non-PC) *Book of Common Prayer* puts it, stand ready "to do good to all men, according to our abilities and opportunities." But the real change must come from within. And unless they do it soon, it may be too late.

Perhaps it already is. Perhaps some peoples, some nations, may even choose deliberately not to sacrifice what they have, culturally and socially, in order to embrace the new world. Perhaps they'll live. Perhaps they'll even prosper as adjuncts and backwaters of the age. But they'll neither participate in nor fully share the quantum leaps of the twenty-first century.

Increasingly, however, they'll be able to destroy those quantum leaps, and much else besides. Increasingly, they will have access to and use WMD: Weapons of Mass Destruction (nuclear and enhanced conventional explosives); mass death (chemical and biological weapons); and mass disruption (cyberwar). Perhaps they'll also try agroterrorism, the deliberate destruction of crops and of the ability to produce food: no small peril on a planet with ever more mouths to feed, ever less decent farmland, and ever fewer kinds of crops to cultivate. Perhaps their weapons will even let loose forces virulent enough to trash the planet.

Which brings us to the subject of the planet, the stage on which all this will transpire. It is not a neutral stage, a mere proscenium on which we humans fret and strut. The planet has always been an active, sometimes a decisive player in the affairs of humankind, although ever since the Industrial Revolution (or was it the Enlightenment?) the West has done its best to ignore the fact. But Nature cannot be ignored forever. Nature acts on her own. Nature responds to what we do, and not always for the better from the human perspective. Pay me now or pay me later. The Wars of the Ways will take place amid a set of inter-related and inter-acting natural and man-made catastrophes—of new plagues and diseases; of famine; of rampant overpopulation in the areas that can least afford it; of ecological havoc in the areas that can least afford it; and quite possibly, ecological havoc everywhere. It is at the least conceivable that these factors and others will combine to threaten the very survival of humanity and the habitability of the planet. Ecocide: the degradation of the environment to the point of catastrophic collapse. History is filled with examples of tribes and empires doing just that.

Yes, legions of environmental apocalyptics have worked these themes to death over the past fifty years. Yes, there's been a lot of over-hyped junk science, and a lot of equally junky refutation. And yes, it's easy to sneer that we needn't worry since, according to the 1970s prognostications of Paul Ehrlich and the Club of Rome, we all starved to death ten years ago. But ecological change—natural and human—is an ineluctable fact of life. And to quote a contemporary American sage, "Don't think it won't happen just because it hasn't happened yet."[2]

Such will be the twenty-first century. Enormous promise. Enormous peril. As I write these words and look over at the other computer, the day's dispatches (in more modern parlance, e-mail) bring me two brief items, significant because they seem so ordinary they barely catch my attention. Some Israelis have invented a "DNA" nanocomputer made out of biochemicals that, if perfected, would be billions of times faster than present inorganic models. And four Palestinian children were killed when one of them kicked an unexploded Israeli tank shell and it detonated. Each side had the usual things to say about the other.

So it goes. Enormous potential. Enormous peril. What to do in such a world? I've suggested that it must be the American purpose to serve as a guardian (certainly not the only guardian) of the twenty-first century, and that we must create a military capable of what the Pentagon calls "full spectrum dominance"—the ability to prevail in whatever forms of conflict the Wars of the Ways might require. I believe that we are a people capable of doing it. But we must be clear about the world in which we fight, as well as about our enemies and ourselves.

We've sketched the nature of the enemy. Now a bit about the world. Then, before getting into the military aspects, a meditation of sorts on the quintessentially American search for "Purpose."

---

2. Jackson Browne, "The Road and the Sky," *Late for the Sky,* Asylum/Elektra Records, 1974.

AGAINST ALL TERRORS

The World as It Is

To most Americans, the Wasted Nineties seemed a decade of historically unprecedented national prosperity. In many ways, it was. But as with all prosperous eras, after a while the genuine accomplishments begin to generate, then give way to the transient excesses. The computers remain. The dot.coms and the IPO babies, and the liquidity they soaked up and squandered, do not. To most Americans, the Wasted Nineties seemed a decade of unprecedented global prosperity. In many ways, it was. Global output rose from $31 trillion in 1990 to $42 trillion in 2000: a performance not likely to be repeated any time soon. But it was a prosperity far more vulnerable to cyclical swings and outright collapse than America's. Long before 9/11, there were Russian and Asian and Latin American financial meltdowns; a Japanese economy mired in chronic stagnation; a European Union with troubles of its own. Then came America's recession, with predictable effects worldwide. When America sneezes, so runs the cliché, the world catches cold. Or worse.

And there were the poor, legatees of a prosperity ever more unevenly distributed, for reasons ranging from natural disasters and war to governmental corruption and (most of all) lack of the kind of ordered freedom that allows people to create. According to Niall Ferguson, an Oxford professor of financial history: "In the 1960s, the richest fifth of the world's population had a total income 30 times as great as the poorest fifth's; in 1998, the ratio was 74:1."[3] Today, over a billion people still live on less than $1 a day, and nearly three billion on less than $2 a day, often under conditions of anarchy and with minimal access to food, water, shelter.[4]

Their numbers are growing, both absolutely and as a percentage of the whole. Today there are over six billion of us, up from three billion in 1960. Current projections offer a range of 7.9 to 10.9 billion of us by 2050.[5] This represents a significant downward revision from the more alarmist predictions of recent decades, which ran as high as 16 billion. A fifty year orgy of contraception, abortion, and infanticide contributed to the abatement, along with the usual horrors of

---

3. Niall Ferguson, "Four Trends Shaping the Early Twenty-First Century," *New York Times Magazine,* 2 December 2001, Early Bird.
4. See WorldWatch Institute, *State of the World 2001* (New York: Norton, 2002), pp. 4, 7.
5. United Nations, *The State of the World Population 2001,* at www.unfpa.org.

war, famine, and disease. But if the history of the West is any guide, population stabilization occurs only after development. It follows prosperity. It does not cause it. And it grows ever more doubtful that much of the world can achieve the level of development necessary for a "natural" stabilization.

Cities are usually equated, and rightly, with the production of freedom and wealth. But in much of the underdeveloped world, cities generate mostly poverty, desperation, and the criminality and violence born of both. Unfortunately, this world's becoming increasingly urbanized as older social structures break down and people leave their farms and villages. By some estimates, half the world's poor population will live in urban areas by 2050—hideous megasprawls where government fails and the hatred and fanaticism born of despair metastasize.

And this population will be young. In the Middle East, for example, over half the Islamic population is under 25.[6] Of all the forces making for radicalism and violence, few can equal the ferocity of youth with no stake, no hope, and no respect for the world that oppresses them.

There will also be resource struggles: ever more furious competition for oil, land, food. But the greatest chronic crisis of the twenty-first century may involve water—too little in some places, too much in others. Barring major technological breakthroughs, i.e., a cheap way to desalinate sea water, the world's physical supply of fresh water is essentially static. By 2025, half the world's population will be living under conditions of chronic water shortage, often because of war and governmental mismanagement, but often because the water simply ain't there. Much of this shortage will occur in areas already predisposed to violence for other reasons, especially the Middle East and central Asia. Afghanistan, for example, has gone through years of drought. Even under conditions of stable peace, water rights and usage would roil the relations of Israel, Palestine, Syria, Jordan, and Lebanon.

And by the by, the Earth's ice may be melting. Ironically, the greatest water problem of the twenty-first century may be too much, and you don't have to be an ecological prophet of doom to understand the possible consequences. Whether this shrinkage of glaciers and ice

---

6. Elaine Sciolino, "Radicalism: Is the Devil in the Details?" *New York Times,* 9 December 2001, Early Bird.

packs is caused by natural and cyclical forces, by human activity, or most likely by a combination, is immaterial here. Melting ice may mean rising sea levels. It's not a simple equation. Many other factors, from increased vegetation to solar and geophysical cycles, enter in. Nonetheless, half the world's population and most of its wealth is found within a hundred miles of some shore. The West may have more to lose, but the rest of the world will suffer more.

If the Wasted Nineties seemed to most Americans a decade of unprecedented prosperity, they also seemed a decade of unprecedented peace. There was, of course, that mess in the Balkans. There were a few other spots that the TV cameras could reach, when the networks chose to send them. There was Rwanda, and some other places in Africa, where the cameras dared not go. Still, the Cold War was over. *We* were at peace. And much of what was going on we didn't need to consider "real" war because, to our eyes, it didn't look like "real" war.

But SIPRI, the Stockholm International Peace Research Institute, which keeps track of global conflict, offers a different perspective. SIPRI defines a major armed conflict as: "the use of armed force between the military forces of two or more governments, or of one government and at least one organized armed group, resulting in the battle-related deaths of at least 1,000 people in any single year and in which the incompatibility concerns control of government and/or territory." Not an entirely exhaustive definition. Still, according to their count, the decade began with 32 conflicts and ended with 27. The most peaceful year, 1997, saw only 19 such.[7]

What might such wars be about? The Western perspective holds that wars are fought between states and involve something called "interests." Economic and territorial interests especially. Certainly, the most publicized fracas of the decade, the Gulf War, was about precisely that. But some scholars and experts discerned other, more ancient patterns, emerging and re-emerging.

A few astute fellows, from Henry Kissinger to Charles Krauthammer, pointed out that rigid, enduring power balances—Superpower against Superpower, bloc against bloc—were relative historical anomalies.[8] Far more common was the dynamic balance.

---

7. *SIPRI, The Study of Armed Conflicts and Their Prevention, 2000,* at www.sipri.org.
8. For an astute analysis, see Charles Krauthammer, "The Real New World Order," *Weekly Standard,* 12 November 2001, Internet.

Whenever a hegemonic power emerged, the other powers within the system banded together against it, with or without a dominant power to orchestrate the opposition. The goodness or evil of the hegemon mattered less than its power. Nations pursue their own ends and, like people, don't usually care to be overshadowed, no matter how benignly. On a planet with nearly 200 nation-states (the number keeps growing), it was inevitable that multitudes of more or less anti-American arrangements—some active and formal, others restricted to communities of *ressentiment*; some single-issue, some more complex—would emerge.

Yet other analysts noticed that, if old types of power relationship were re-emerging, so were old, indeed ancient, patterns of conflict. Martin van Crevald, an Israeli military historian with a devoted American following, came out in 1991 with *The Transformation of War*. His thesis was simple. "We are entering an era, not of peaceful economic competition between trading blocks, but of warfare between ethnic and religious groups. Even as familiar forms of armed conflict are sinking into the dustbin of the past, radically new ones are raising their heads ready to take their place."[9]

Van Crevald didn't contend, as his critics have sometimes complained, that inter-state conventional warfare was either totally obsolete or no longer possible. Indeed, the Gulf War occurred only a few months after the book's publication. He did, however, argue that the nation-state's *de facto* monopoly of significant violence was at an end, and that the things for which groups fought would once again encompass far more than the "rational" goals of states. "As marriage has not always been concluded for love, so war has not always been waged for 'interest.'"[10] War would continue to be waged for territory, for resources, for other tangible advantages. But war would also be waged, once again, for the sake of ethnicity, tribe, religion, race, and often enough for the sheer thrill of it. Especially for the young.

Others sensed the changes. In a 1993 *Foreign Affairs* article later expanded into a best-selling book, *The Clash of Civilizations*, Harvard political scientist Samuel P. Huntington developed the notion that future war would involve far more than Western-style states fighting for Western-style "rational" interests. He even suggested that

9. Martin van Crevald, *The Transformation of War* (New York: Free Press, 1991), p. viii.
10. Ibid, p. 212.

twentieth century notions of First, Second, and Third Worlds were no longer valid. "It is far more meaningful now to group countries not in terms of their political or economic systems or in terms of their level of economic development but rather in terms of their culture and civilization. . . . The fault lines between civilizations will be the battle lines of the future."[11]

Even Huntington wasn't sure how many actors there would be. He designated "seven or eight major civilizations. These include Western, Confucian, Japanese, Islamic, Hindu, Slavic-Orthodox, Latin American and possibly African civilization."[12] Many of these would have "core states" that would lead coalitions in "fault line wars" that might get exceedingly ugly, but could rarely be settled definitively, since they involved matters of cultural identity as well as territory and other quantifiable interests. Many of the wars of the nineties, he went on, might be described as "transition wars" in which the cultural elements were present, but not yet dominant—or at least not dominant to Western minds. How many of the wars of the nine-ties exhibited such characteristics? Hard to say. Probably, more than half. Perhaps only the African wars—a set of conflicts that experts have taken to calling "Africa's First World War"—and a couple Mid-dle Eastern conflicts might be excluded. Even Desert Storm, begun as a purely local real estate grab, ended as a "fault line war" of sorts.

Huntington also noticed two forces that intensified the push toward inter-cultural wars. One was obvious. "In class and ideologi-cal conflicts, the key question was 'Which side are you on?' and peo-ple could and did choose sides and change sides. In conflicts between civilizations, the question is 'What are you?' That is a given that can-not be changed." But he also discerned something more complex. "A de-Westernization and indigenization of elites is occurring in many non-Western countries at the same time that Western, usually Ameri-can, cultures, styles and habits become more popular among the masses of the people."[13]

This is vital. For the past couple centuries, one of the great mixed blessings of the non-Western world was the extent to which indige-nous élites identified themselves with Western culture and com-

---

11. Samuel P. Huntington, "The Clash of Civilizations?" *Foreign Affairs* (Summer 1993), at www.foreignaffairs.com. See also Samuel P. Huntington, *The Clash of Civilizations and the Remaking of World Order* (New York: Touchstone, 1996).
12. Huntington, "The Clash of Civilizations?"
13. Ibid.

merce. They went to European and American schools, worked for and with Western interests, lived Western-style lives, and felt utterly estranged from the masses of their own people . . . who often felt the same way about them. But now, as shards of Western culture and a considerable tonnage of consumer goods percolate down to the masses, the situation reverses. The élites, often still Western-educated and attuned to Western ways, grow angry at the perceived trashing of their culture, and find themselves doubly alienated. More importantly, so do the children of the élites. The men who did 9/11, and many of their colleagues around the world, fit this description perfectly.

Not everyone accepted Huntington's diagnosis. Some felt that he paid insufficient attention to intra-civilization wars (as though this made the world more peaceful). Thomas L. Friedman, a *New York Times* columnist, argued that the globalization of the masses that Huntington feared would take some of the edge off the fault lines. In his best-seller, *The Lexus and the Olive Tree,* he even offered, not entirely facetiously, his "Golden Arches Theory of Human Conflict," noting that there had never (yet) been a war between two countries after they both got their first McDonald's. But he also understood that globalization could produce a nasty backlash, certainly among the nations that couldn't keep up, and also among the peoples who found the competition and the products both vile and evil. And he spoke of a future in which "super-empowered angry men" would take actions which some would find vile, evil, and incomprehensible, but which others would celebrate as a splendid and justified response to the real and perceived evils of American economic and military dominance and cultural toxicity.

And one man, perhaps, saw it coming most clearly of all. For the last three decades, Robert Kaplan has covered the world. His books, especially *Balkan Ghosts* and *The Ends of the Earth,* combine brilliant travel writing with astute analysis. In a 1994 *Atlantic Monthly* article, "The Coming Anarchy," he laid it out:

> To understand the events of the next fifty years, then, one must understand environmental scarcity, cultural and racial clash, geographic destiny, and the transformation of war. . . .
>
> We are entering a bifurcated world. Part of the globe is inhabited by . . . [those] healthy, well fed, and pampered by technology.

The other, larger, part, is inhabited by . . . [those] condemned to a life that is "poor, nasty, brutish, and short.". . .

Economic modernization is not necessarily a panacea, since it fuels individual and group ambitions while weakening traditional loyalties to the state. . . . [The world approaches] an epoch of theme-less juxtapositions, in which the classificatory grid of nation-states is going to be replaced by a jagged-glass pattern of city-states, shanty-states, nebulous and anarchic regionalisms . . .[14]

And in another article, "Was Democracy Just a Moment?" he demolished one of America's most cherished beliefs about its Purpose in the world. "I submit that the democracy we are encouraging in many poor parts of the world is an integral part of a transformation toward new forms of authoritarianism. . . If a society is not in reasonable health, democracy can be not only risky but disastrous . . ."[15]

Finally, in his most recent book, *Warrior Politics,* (written before 9/11) Kaplan predicted Operation Enduring Freedom, the Afghan campaign. "The bipolar nature of World War II and Cold War alliances is no longer evident. Our situation is more similar to that of the late Victorians, who had to deal with nasty little wars in anarchic corners of the globe, such as Sudan [and its charismatic Islamic warrior/ leader, the Mahdi]. Is it too far-fetched to imagine our own expedition through similar desert wastes to apprehend another Mahdi-like figure, Osama bin Laden?"[16]

It has come to pass. The philosopher George Santayana once remarked that those who do not know history are condemned to repeat it. Santayana got it wrong. Those who know history repeat it. Those who do not know history are condemned to be surprised when it happens.

But history often repeats in novel ways. In the twenty-first century, these ancient forms of war will be waged with a twist which, via van Crevald and others, has become known as "The Revenge of the Melians." In 416 BCE, as recorded in Thucydides' *Peloponnesian War,* Athens attempted to coerce the tiny island of Melos into an alliance of subservience. When the Melians refused and invoked a moral

14. See Robert D. Kaplan, "The Coming Anarchy," in *The Coming Anarchy: Shattering the Dreams of the Post Cold War World* (New York: Vintage, 2000), pp. 3–57.
15. Ibid, pp. 60, 62.
16. Robert D. Kaplan, *Warrior Politics: Why Leadership Demands a Pagan Ethos* (New York: Random House, 2002), pp. 25–26.

right of neutrality, the Athenian delegation replied: "Right, as the world goes, is only in question between equals in power. The strong do what they wish and the weak suffer what they must." However, given the spread of terrorism, concluded van Crevald, "At certain levels of engagement, 'It is the weak who do what they can, the strong who suffer what they must.'"[17]

And throughout the Wasted Nineties, we put up with a great deal. The first World Trade Center bombing in 1993. The Khobar Towers bombing of 1996. The African embassy bombings in 1998. The U.S.S. *Cole* in 2000. A hundred other minor incidents, often not publicly reported or considered worth the bother of public reporting. Throughout the decade, indeed, ever since the Iranian hostage crisis of 1979–1981, our response was invariably the same. Harsh rhetoric, an occasional trial, an occasional salvo of precision-guided something or other . . . a lot of sound and fury, signifying that it was OK to attack the World's Sole Remaining Superpower. After all, we knew that we were the World's Sole Remaining Superpower, and nothing was going to change that, and we were in love with what we'd become, and would remain.

And anyway, terrorism was a global phenomenon. Others had it much worse. Two months before 9/11, Larry Johnson, a former State Department counter-terrorism specialist, assured America that we had little to fear. His *New York Times* op-ed on the subject is worth a bit of quotation:

"Judging from news reports and the portrayal of villains in our popular entertainment, Americans are bedeviled by fantasies about terrorism. They seem to believe that terrorism is the greatest threat to the United States and that it is becoming more widespread and lethal." Mr. Johnson reassured his readers that although incidents were up, fatalities were down. "Nor are the United States and its policies the primary target." Not a single American had died from terrorism so far in 2001. He attributed much of the growing concern to sensationalistic media, and to military and intelligence bureaucracies in need of enemies to justify their budgets. "Terrorism," he concluded, "is not the biggest security challenge confronting the United States, and it should not be portrayed that way."[18]

---

17. Mr. van Crevald apparently first codified the "Revenge of the Melians" in another book, *The Sword and the Olive.* The quote here is taken from Kenneth F. McKenzie, Jr., *The Revenge of the Melians: Asymmetric Threats and the Next QDR,* McNair Paper #62 (Washington, DC: National Defense University, 2001), pp. ix, 4.

AGAINST ALL TERRORS

Well, as Zeus once said to Narcissus: Watch yourself.

The "Purpose" Debate

We were enamored. Self-enamored. And throughout the Wasted Nineties, there raged and sputtered a debate of sorts over America's "Purpose" now that we'd become omnipotent. Today, that debate might charitably be described as inane. There's no need here to critique it in depth. Still, it matters. For when you parse it, you get a sense of a terrible, indeed a tragic American flaw. Call it ethnocentricity, call it solipsism, call it arrogance. The essence of it is: We don't have to understand the world. We already know about us.

The main bout of the Purpose Debate featured the "America's Greatness" crowd against the "Muscular Humanitarians." The former faction, centered around a few conservative and neo-conservative think tanks and a couple magazines more renowned for their influence than for their circulation, argued for "the cause of American leadership" . . . as though American leadership were in itself a cause.[19] America must lead because America must lead, regardless of who was or was not following. Some labeled them "American Gaullists." Charles de Gaulle, France's World War II hero and later president, had oft proclaimed that France without greatness wasn't France, To the American Gaullists, America without greatness—read here, global hegemony, globally and exuberantly enforced—wasn't really America.

Arrayed against them, but often in *de facto* alliance, were the Muscular Humanitarians. When the Clinton administration's other Warrior Princess, Secretary of State Madeleine Albright, proclaimed America "the indispensable nation," they agreed.[20] But where the America's Greatness people cherished power, the Muscular Humanitarians and their Clintonista friends valued benevolence. Historian Loren Baritiz has well summed this mentality: "American nationalism, when its fist clenched, went forth not to pillage but to instruct."[21]

---

18. Larry C. Johnson, "The Declining Terrorist Threat," *New York Times,* 10 July 2001, Early Bird.

19. William Kristol, "Statement of Principles," Project for the New American Century, Fax Memorandum, 3 June 1997.

20. See Madeleine K. Albright, "The Testing of American Foreign Policy," *Foreign Affairs* 77 (November 1998), pp. 50—64.

21. Baritz, *Backfire* (New York: Morrow, 1985), p. 41.

And it didn't start with Madeleine Albright. It goes at least as far back as Woodrow Wilson's determination, first to "teach the Mexicans to elect good men," then to redeem the whole human species after the First World War. It has flowed through every "nation-building" scheme ever since. Baritz calls it the foreign policy of Pygmalion. "We fall in love with what we create."[22] Or with what we think we create.

More often than not, throughout the nineties, these two antagonists found themselves supporting American interventions in the Balkans and elsewhere, albeit for different reasons. That these interventions either failed (Haiti, Somalia) or proved frustratingly interminable (the Balkans) mattered little. Since 9/11, the two sides have diverged in many ways. The former demand lots more violence; the latter, lots more compassion. At the moment, they also seem to be coalescing into what's become known as the "Attack Iraq" crowd. Clearly, they're in agreement on two things. America must always be doing something. And America must never honestly ask itself the international equivalent of a very common adolescent question.

If we're so cute, how come we can't get a date?

Others thought they had the answer. An unlikely congeries of left libertarians and far right isolationists felt that mucking about in other people's domestics was bad for the American body and soul. Neo-populists such as Pat Buchanan demanded that America shed its empire, mend its free-trading/immigrant-welcoming ways, and thereby (*sic*) get its republic back.[23] Left libertarians argued that while America must remain open to the world economically and culturally, "the best defense is to give no offense."[24] John Quincy Adams' dictum that while America wishes all nations well, "she goes not abroad in search of monsters to destroy," became their creed. And some wondered whether American interests and purposes might best be served by backing off a bit. One government study, *Seeking a National Strategy*, even quoted Shakespeare to make the point:

O it is excellent

To have a giant's strength; but it is tyrannous

---

22. Ibid, p. 34.

23. See two works by Patrick J. Buchanan, *The Great Betrayal* (Boston: Little, Brown, 1998) and *A Republic, Not an Empire: Reclaiming America's Destiny* (Washington, DC: Regnery, 1999).

24. See Ivan Eland, "Protecting the Homeland: The Best Defense Is to Give No Offense," *Cato Policy Analysis* #306, Cato Institute, at www.cato.org.

AGAINST ALL TERRORS

To use it like a giant.[25]

In retrospect, two things stand out about the Purpose Debate. Nobody really seemed all that interested in the complexities of the world, or how the world might experience us. Those who did were generally dismissed as either left-wing, Blame America Firsties or somehow lacking in "nerve." To repeat, the post-Cold War America's Purpose debate wasn't about the world. It was about us, and all the dandy things that we could do for the world, whether the world wanted them or not.

And despite all the rhetorical alarms and the occasional real-world explosion, it was a debate conducted amid a fine, serene, and utterly delusional sense of safety. As one of the great clichés of the Wasted Nineties proclaimed, "The [Russian] bear may be gone, but the woods are still full of snakes." However, few of the protagonists expected anything like a serious, let alone mortal challenge to emerge. Some, almost wistfully, cited China; others, a renascent Iran or Iraq. Some worried about a Russia gone rogue or a North Korea gone ballistic. Many fretted over the proliferation of some nasty weaponry, or the steady growth of terror networks in faraway places with strange-sounding and sometimes rapidly changing names. But clearly, no "peer competitor," no Axis or Warsaw Pact, was in the offing. And when much of the rhetoric of threat got tied to calls for promiscuous increases in defense spending—the Purpose crowd has never met a weapon it didn't like—the alarms, alas, proved all too easy to downplay or dismiss.[26] In some ways, counter-terrorism expert Larry Johnson (who became a post 9/11 television commentator) wasn't all that wrong about some of the fretting going on.

In short, *we* could argue so strenuously about us and our Purposes because *they* were either comparatively weak or intrinsically unimportant. At times, they—the snakes—almost seemed abstractions, convenient to invoke but not taken all that seriously. The world was ours to mold in our own image, provided only we had the nerve, or the compassion, or both. That most of the world felt profoundly

---

25. *U.S. Commission on National Security/Twenty-First Century, Seeking a National Strategy* (Washington, DC: GPO, 2000), p. 15.

26. It's important to distinguish here between those advocating "the cause of American leadership" and those who, throughout the nineties, worked tirelessly to alert America to the imminent dangers. Sometimes the two efforts overlapped. But the *leitmotif* of the Purpose Debate was egocentricity, not peril.

uncomfortable with, or hostile to, our pretensions—well, that too could be fixed.

Throughout the nineties, then, as we scavenged for a Purpose in the world, that world was changing radically. Among nation-states, comfortable rigidities were giving way to new fluidities. At the same time, the dominance of nation-states in world affairs was beginning to erode. Globalization was bringing it about economically; armed and ruthless transnational and subnational political movements were bringing it about militarily. Indeed, without globalization, without its transportation and communications technologies and financial structures, Al Qaeda would have remained at best a nasty curiosity, and Osama bin Laden a very unfunny joke.

But we were like adolescents. It wasn't that we didn't know. It was that we didn't want to know, or didn't care to draw the appropriate conclusions. Self-image mattered more.

What Purpose Now?

By December 11th, 2001, three months after the catastrophe, the Taliban barely governed a few final caves. The victors were squabbling and sniping among themselves. Historically, such rapid advances have the norm in Afghan fighting, as much the norm as pre-surrender side-switching and post-victory fratricide. Before departing Kandahar for points unknown, Mullah Omar, head of the Taliban, threatened the "extinction" of the United States. Mr. bin Laden, whereabouts at the time also unknown, more or less claimed possession of nuclear and chemical weapons. Americans were all relieved that the crash of the American Airlines Airbus in New York was "only" an accident, although nobody was really sure, since that item dropped off the media play list a few days after the disaster. After several national alerts, reports began circulating that Something Big was planned for the United Nations: a suitcase nuke perhaps, or else maybe some germs. And airline passengers started taking off their shoes.

So it went. So it is. So it will be. What Purpose now? For now is the time, if ever there was one, to define a Purpose. This is no longer merely about us, about our preferences, our self-image and other delusions. It's about us in a world that both hates us and needs us.

The United States of America has a Purpose in this world, but only if we can see it clearly. It should be the American mission to serve as a defender, a steward, a guardian of the twenty-first century, on behalf of a world that, more often than not, will despise and condemn us for it. It is a matter of survival, of self-interest (enlightened and non), and of moral obligation. We'll not be the only defender, of course, not the only guardian. But we are the only one with the military power to mount the defense, and to aid and co-ordinate the defenses of others, when and as appropriate. The military aspect is only one part of guardianship, but it is also the precondition for the others. War will be necessary; war may be chronic. Without military success, other endeavors must ultimately fail.

But what is success? I suggest that, over the next few years, military success might be defined roughly as follows.

Today, the United States is at war with a nation you won't find on any map. Call it "Jihadistan" or more conventionally, the "arc of terror" that runs from northern and central Africa through the Middle East, up into central Asia and western China, thence to Southeast Asia, the Philippines, Indonesia. Via the Islamic diaspora, Jihadistan now holds outposts throughout western Europe and the Americas. The most obvious goals of Jihadistan are the destruction of Israel; the expulsion of all foreigners and especially Americans from Islamic lands; the resurrection of the *Umma,* the Islamic world living under *Shar'ia,* strict Islamic law; and the propagation of their brand of Islam beyond those borders. Taliban Afghanistan was only one province of Jihadistan, and Al Qaeda only one faction.

Jihadistan must be destroyed as a force capable of practicing and exporting terror. Ultimately, how the Islamic world arranges its affairs must be its own business. Whether or not Jihadistan can wreak its destruction worldwide, whether or not it can torment the world economically, is our business. Jihadistan must not under any circumstances be permitted to possess, let alone use, weapons of mass destruction, mass death, or mass disruption. Here Jihadistan includes hostile fundamentalist nations, hostile fundamentalist groups, and "secular" regimes such as Iraq and Syria, which support them. (When "world opinion" and the "world community" warn against action against Iran or Iraq, are they saying that they actually want them to possess WMD?) The United States must be prepared to take whatever actions we deem necessary, unilaterally or in concert with others, to prevent these groups and states from acquiring, producing, or employing these weapons against anybody. This protection must extend to non-*Jehadi* Islamic states, present and future.

The destruction of Jihadistan may take decades. Meanwhile, an array of other issues will engage the United States. An independent Palestine must come to pass. The prospect of the Al Aqsa Intifada (now more aptly called a Palestinian-Israeli civil war) escalating into a regional conflict where both sides use WMD is utterly unacceptable. The United States must impose—yes, impose—an interim settlement that will separate these two peoples. In all probability, a large American peace-keeping and peace-enforcing presence will be required. One Army study estimates about 20,000. Other nations, perhaps Canada, the European Union, and especially Turkey, may and should contribute. But the burden will be primarily ours.

Beyond the Middle East, a half-dozen Asian conflicts simmer and seethe: India versus Pakistan, China versus Taiwan, North Korea versus South Korea, to name only the most prominent. For centuries, Asian conflicts were limited by distance, terrain, and vegetation; Asian armies simply couldn't get at each other very well. But most of the Asian arms buildup these last few decades has involved naval and air forces, and missiles. These countries can now do each other serious harm, and their individual conflicts may well escalate into regional and global confrontations, including the use of WMD.[27]

Finally, there's the African tragedy; the present and probable future destabilization of much of Latin America; narco-terrorism; and an endless array of subnational and transnational crazies, from violent racists and anarchists to eco-terrorists. These too may have their military aspects.

Of course, it is always better to let those involved settle their own conflicts. Whenever possible, other nations and organizations should provide the necessary forces. Currently, few nations possess such forces. Therefore, the United States should support European Union and Russian attempts to create regional Rapid Reaction Forces. America needs to learn how to let others be strong, and that sometimes the best form of "leadership" is to get out of the way. But that may not always be possible. The basic approach should be to commit

---

27. For an excellent assessment of the Asian situation see Paul Bracken, *Fire in the East: The Rise of Asian Military Power and the Second Nuclear Age* (New York: HarperCollins, 1999).

AGAINST ALL TERRORS

American forces only to deal with problems that other organizations and arrangements can't handle, and then with clear and decisive intent, and with the support of an American people that clearly understands both the stakes and how the military works.

And then get out and let other, less encumbered nations and organizations put their people on the ground.

But we are a nation of military illiterates. No one has been drafted since the early seventies. Ever fewer veterans serve in government. National defense is not exactly a popular subject on campus. And although defense journalism has improved markedly over the last decade, it still concentrates far too much on sound bites; on breathless disquisitions on all that high-tech gadgetry; and on talking head "experts" whose commentary seem to follow a predictable pattern: The more they're paid, the less they say. So how to engage the American intellect? And, even more important, how to re-engage the American people to participate in the common defense as a routine matter of citizenship?

The next chapter deals with America's military, as it is today. The chapter after that considers what must be done, and the relationship of the citizenry to those needs. Then to a final chapter with some brief thoughts on how to become a people who can sustain the Wars of the Ways.

CHAPTER

2

The Wasted
Nineties

Economists have a phrase for one of the most ubiquitous aspects of modern life. "Rational ignorance." We're busy. The world's complex. There are many things that affect us, which we cannot affect, at least not directly. In such cases, it's not worth our time to study them. We're ignorant because we're powerless and because other things matter more to us.

On September 10th, 2001, national defense fell into this category for most Americans. On September 11th, it did not. Since then, we've been supplied with endless snippets of information, misinformation, and disinformation from the media and their on-call experts, as well as the good folks at the Pentagon. We've been filled with sound bites and telegenic fury, signifying more or less nothing. We lack larger context. We've allowed ourselves to become a nation of military illiterates. And we've been told incessantly that there's this awful culture gap, this dangerous estrangement, between the military "caste" and the people.[1] Finally, the whole subject's awfully complex, even for veterans. It's like someone with a basic liberal arts education trying to understand the nuances of cancer and the intricacies of treatment. Hardly worth the effort.

Unless, of course, you or someone you care about has been diagnosed. Then it's astonishing how smart you can get, and how fast.

The American people need to get smart about things military. We need to do it now. For national defense is not simply something the government does for us. Government's the agent only. We the People are ultimately responsible for providing for the common defense, a providing that may take many forms at many levels. Defense is more than a task we can pay others to perform. It's also more than an obligation. It's a right, one we exercise both individually and collectively. And in fact, the basic issues are eminently comprehensible.

Several years ago, former Senator and Democratic presidential aspirant Gary Hart, a veteran defense reformer, put it well:

> [T]here is nothing—*nothing*—in the whole framework of military policy and practice that any American of ordinary intelligence cannot understand. Concerned citizens—and we should all be con-

---

1. During the latter Clinton years, a large academic and popular literature on this civil-military "estrangement" poured forth. Since 9/11, no one has mentioned it. In fact, the "estrangement" notion has taken its place alongside another historic civil-military curiosity: the "nuclear fear" that a variety of left-wing psychiatrists and psychologists used to allege was destroying the minds and morals of our nation. When the Soviet Union collapsed, so did "nuclear fear."

cerned—can demand an explanation as to why our forces are structured as they are, why they are equipped one way rather than another, and, most of all, why they should be sent here or there in the world. It boils down to common sense, which can be found at least as readily on Main Street as on Pennsylvania Avenue.[2]

At least.

The Premise

In a previous world, that on the other side of 9/11, America's military needs were different. Or so we've come to believe. At the moment, most of the emphasis is on what it takes to root out the Islamic *Jehadi*: special and unconventional ground forces, air power, intelligence. And most of the rest is on homeland defense, especially against WMD, weapons of mass destruction, death, and disruption. This is certainly understandable. But the Wars of the Ways will require the full array of American power, and that array must be utterly transformed if it is to prevail.

Indeed, the current situation is unprecedented in world history. The United States must transform its present forces, technologically, structurally, and operationally, while fighting a new kind—no, several different new kinds—of war (new to us, at any rate). President Bush described this challenge a bit hyperbolically, but nonetheless aptly during a December 2001 speech: "It's like overhauling an engine while you're going 80 miles an hour. Yet we have no other choice." Mr. Bush was emphatic. Transformation will go on with "a new sense of urgency."[3]

But what exactly is transformation? Like beauty or your 1040 deductions, it's often more in the eye of the beholder than an objectively definable condition. For our purposes (and please pardon a bit of Pentagonese; it's necessary from time to time), we'll call it an open-ended process of creating, adapting, and developing military technologies, organizations, doctrines, and operations in a manner that renders them effective against the current and probable array of threats. What makes this historically new is the velocity of change. Once, militaries might remain fundamentally unaltered for ages.

---

2. Gary Hart, *The Minuteman: Restoring an Army of the People* (New York: Free Press, 1998), p. 53.

3. "President Speaks on War Effort to Citadel Cadets," White House press release/ Transcript, 11 December 2001, at www.whitehouse.gov.

AGAINST ALL TERRORS

Medieval catapults weren't all that different from, and were in some ways inferior to, Roman models a millennium before. The infantry rifle took centuries to evolve. Most of the major American systems now in use were designed in the sixties and seventies. Now we must look to radical changes in years, even months. Can it be done? Yes, it can. For the Wasted Nineties were a time of both neglect and preparation, of frustration and of hope.

Epiphany

Not so very long ago, in 1998, the Joint Chiefs of Staff (JCS) did a curious thing. After years of denying that the military had any serious problems, years of dismissing the cumulating evidence as "anecdotal" or "anomalous" or "an insult to our young men and women in uniform," they asked for more money. Of itself, this was hardly curious. After all, the Beltway measures success at least as much by input as by output. But the way they did it was a bit unusual. They trooped up to Capitol Hill for a series of pre-arranged, well-publicized committee hearings that left their Congressional interrogators in a state of artfully contrived, hyperventilated rage, both for having been "lied to" by the Pentagon for all these years, and over the condition of America's defenses in general.

Had Congress been deceived? Only if you believe that they had no other sources of information than the Clinton Pentagon's official line, which they'd naively accepted as Holy Writ for the preceding five years. In truth, the opposite had prevailed. Everybody knew that the military was on the verge of implosion. The hearings, a scripted counterpoint of "revelation" and "shock," were intended to juice up the appropriations process, to start pumping more billions into an establishment that already consumed over $300 billion a year.[4] Everybody knew that the weapons and equipment were aging; that maintenance was abysmal; that things and people were wearing out;

---

4. The Defense Department has its own budget "line item," but many other agencies are involved in national security. Part of the nuclear budget goes to the Energy Department. Then there's the intelligence community and a variety of other functions scattered through the government. Also, it's important to distinguish between "authorization" and "appropriation." These are separate procedures, one authorizing money to be spent, the other actually providing it. For any given year, the two may differ by tens of billions. And then there are the inevitable "supplementals."

and that the present force could not be sustained, let alone modernized on any conceivable peacetime budget.

How much more was needed? Estimates ran from $10 to $100 billion annually, depending on assumptions, parameters, models, wish lists, phases of the moon, etc. Nobody knew. Nobody could know, given a Defense Department accounting system that might fairly be described as surrealistic. A year later, in 1999, Pentagon accountants made almost $7 *trillion* in "adjustments" to their ledgers in a vain attempt to make them balance, but lacked receipts for over $2.3 trillion.[5] All anybody knew was: It was bad.

The hearings had their desired effect. Soon enough, the Clinton administration programmed a steady increase in defense spending: about $227 billion worth from Fiscal Years (FY) 2001–2005, i.e., after Clinton left office. But it wasn't soon enough for the 2000 elections. In his acceptance speech at the Republican National Convention, George W. Bush proclaimed, "Help is on the way." His running mate, former Defense Secretary Dick Cheney, expanded the theme throughout the campaign in his usual calm, no-nonsense, inexorable manner. When President-elect Bush named another former defense secretary, Donald Rumsfeld, to head the Pentagon, it seemed to many that help was indeed on the way—a Reagan-style "Just Spend It" infusion of cash that would quickly repair, refurbish, reinvigorate.

It didn't quite happen that way. In January 2001, the Bush administration announced that there wold be no quick, dramatic spending hikes; the final Clinton budget (FY 2002) of about $302–310 billion, depending on how measured, would stand. For the next nine months, Secretary Rumsfeld and a klatch of *ad hoc* in-house study groups (and a lot of other people) worried the problems. No more cash until Mr. Rumsfeld decided how to spend it. Help was indeed on the way, but not the kind that the Pentagon had expected . . . or wanted. So secretive were the study groups that nobody was publicly sure even how many there were; estimates ranged from a dozen or so to over twenty. So secretive were the reports that the media filled with critiques of some that hadn't even been written. But it slowly became clear that Mr. Rumsfeld planned to do more than repair and beef up the military. He intended nothing less than to drag this creaking,

---

5. "Pentagon's Finances in Disarray," AP Wire Report, 3 March 2000. A year later, the situation had improved somewhat. The GAO found that the Pentagon had only made $1.1 trillion of unjustified and/or undocumented entries.

AGAINST ALL TERRORS

wasteful, Industrial Age behemoth into the twenty-first century. He meant to transform it, and to redeem it thereby.

The first major set of decisions were to be made in fall 2001. By September, the leaks, authorized and not, had pretty much sketched the general contours of what transformation might entail, and the ferocity of internal opposition had become apparent. Transformation required cuts and reallocations. Nobody knew what they might get out of transformation, but everybody had a pretty good—and often artfully exaggerated—sense of what they might lose. Army divisions. Navy carriers. Air Force squadrons. A long list of weapons and systems, all deemed vital by somebody or other. Mr. Rumsfeld, ever unflappable, predicted that, after a rough September, support would "jell" in October.[6]

By October, support had indeed jelled—for quick and massive, deficit-be-damned spending increases for immediate defense needs. Within weeks, the first additional $20 billion made its way to the Pentagon, with $20 billion more in the emergency pipeline and a couple score billion tacked on to the regular budget. Congressional Democrats started falling all over each other to appropriate billions more than President Bush had requested, even when the President stated flatly that they couldn't spend all the money already allotted.[7] And 9/11 found the man who would discipline and transform the defense establishment first out in the hallway helping the injured, then accepting that the rest of his tenure, perhaps of his life, would be dominated by the war that 9/11 had brought home.

In August, Mr. Rumsfeld had described his immediate plans for transformation as limited. That same month, Deputy Defense Secretary Paul Wolfowitz suggested that "If we could achieve a 15 percent transformation in 10 years, I would consider that reasonable."[8]

No more. Today the United States must attempt something virtually unprecedented in world history: making fundamental changes in military structure, armament, doctrine, and operations *while fighting*

6. Vernon Loeb and Walter Pincus, "Rumsfeld: New Strategy Near," *Washington Post*, 23 August 2001, p. A-1.
7. John D. McKinnon and Gary Fields, "Homeland Defense Is Focus of Fight on Budget," *Wall Street Journal*, 3 December 2001, Early Bird.
8. Thom Shanker, "Rumsfeld Says Plans for Military Transformation Are Limited," *New York Times*, 18 August 2001, Early Bird. See also Thom Canahuate, "Total U.S. Military Transformation in 10 Years Not Realistic, Says Wolfowitz," *DefenseNews.com*, 16 August 2001.

several kinds of war. There are many cases on record of military forces, especially defeated military forces, undertaking major reforms in peacetime. Germany between the World Wars comes to mind; in the twenties and thirties, they developed what would later be known as *Blitzkrieg*, or lightning war. There are also examples of modern military forces changing their tactical and operational practices radically in wartime. In 1917, Germany largely abandoned the suicidal mass frontal attacks that had characterized trench warfare, shifted to more fluid tactics, and nearly won the war. During the 1973 Yom Kippur War, Israel changed its tactics to deal with the Egyptians' new anti-tank and anti-air missiles. In the mid-eighties, the USSR abandoned large unit operations in Afghanistan, shifted to rapid airborne small-unit strikes, and nearly won the war; only American Stinger missiles stopped them.

All true. But what America must now do is unique. Power as traditionally structured and measured no longer brings automatic security; technological superiority by itself is meaningless. American power must now be made relevant to the threats we face, made effective against those threats, and made so overpowering that, by its deterrent example, many of the Wars of the Ways won't have to be fought at all.

The Problem of Structure

In the beginning, things were simple. There were armies. There were navies. Armies did land. Navies did water. There were some slight overlaps. Armies might construct shore fortifications and deploy coastal artillery. Navies might occasionally bombard a beach or land small parties of naval infantry, sometimes also known as marines. Still, generally speaking, they had no way to get at each other. And since neither could do the other's job, neither could take the other's job.

The advent of the airplane did more than add a third dimension to warfare. It began to blur the hitherto tidy distinction between land and sea combat. Shore-based aviation could sink ships; ship-based aviation could strike ashore. In addition to airplanes, the twentieth century saw an unprecedented proliferation of other weapons—tanks, missiles, etc.—and the increasing specialization of those systems. Combat aircraft, for example, evolved from the all-purpose biplanes of

World War I into bombers, pursuits, fighters, interceptors, fighter-bombers, attack aircraft, light, medium, and heavy bombers, gunships, and on and on. Artillery, once limited to iron cannonballs, now fires dozens of different rounds and munitions. In World War II, the best anti-tank weapon was another tank, preferably with a bigger main gun (which usually belonged to the Germans or Russians). Today there are maybe twenty ways to kill a tank, theoretically including submarine-launched cruise missiles that disperse satellite or laser-guided submunitions over the battlefield. The "anti-tank submarine" may never be tried, since the boats would have to get a bit too close to shore and it's an ultra-expensive mode of what became known during Desert Storm as "tank plinking." But the point is—when you can fight tanks with submarines, you're in a world of new and, from the organizational and budgetary perspectives, volatile possibilities.

The Afghan campaign has provided a useful example here. The most convenient way to attack Afghanistan, a landlocked country, was from the sea, with aircraft carriers, Marines, and cruise-missile-firing surface ships and submarines—and from the Air Force base on the Indian Ocean island of Diego Garcia.

Further, the twentieth century witnessed an astonishing "mix and match" of weapons and systems. You could now put airplanes on ships: aircraft carriers. You could now put armies on ships: complex large-scale amphibious operations. You could now put armies on airplanes: paratroops and helicopter-borne air assault. You could now put missiles on submarines, surface ships, aircraft, trucks, human shoulders. A hundred more examples might be adduced. This increasing number and specialization of weapons and systems, plus the mix-and-match, has led to one of the defining characteristics of twenty-first century war, whether conventional or counter-terrorist. It might even be called a principle.

Systems proliferate. Effects converge.

In essence, this means that there are now many ways of doing things. Today, the Army and the Navy, not to mention the Air Force and Marines, can do large chunks of each other's jobs. They can, therefore, take large chunks of each other's jobs. Hence one of the most baleful aspects of American military life: inter-service rivalry, endlessly fought over any and all issues that might threaten a service's traditional missions and "core competencies"—and the appropriations they generate.

The present American defense establishment often seems (and in some cases is) willfully designed to exacerbate these tensions. But in the beginning, it was not so. The Preamble to the Constitution speaks of "the common defense," but Article I, Section 8 authorizes Congress to "raise and support Armies" and "provide and maintain a Navy" (evocative wording for different forces with different needs). Subsequent legislation established separate Departments of War and the Navy, with the president as commander-in-chief their only common superior. This arrangement worked reasonably well for the first century and a half. As late as the First World War, the division of labor was clear. The Army went Over There to fight; the Navy ferried them across and kept the sea lanes open. There was little inter-service rivalry, save for the normal Army-Navy Game kinds of things, the Marines against everyone else, and an occasional good-natured barroom brawl.

By the twenties, however, it was obvious that this tidy arrangement couldn't last much longer. Leave aside the Army's chagrin at the Marines' first real success with large-unit, sustained ground combat (Belleau Wood, St. Mihiel, and all that). The problem was the pilots. Air power advocates—perhaps evangelists might be the more appropriate term—in Europe were proclaiming a new doctrine. Future wars, they predicted, could be ended almost as they began by the "strategic bombardment" of enemy cities. No need for armies piled on armies or costly naval armadas. Enemy urban populations, undisciplined and unfit, would panic at the outset, toppling any government that failed to surrender fast enough.

While bombing civilians didn't catch on in America until World War II (and then with a degree of reluctance kept secret until recently), Army enthusiasts such as Billy Mitchell proved that land-based aircraft could sink ships. Unmanned, immobile ships that weren't shooting back, at any rate. In 1933, the Fleet Marine Force was established as a permanent air-ground team capable of long-distance, large-scale operations. The Army didn't take it all that graciously.

During the twenties and thirties, another rivalry, hitherto innocuous, intensified. *Intra*-service—a competition in some ways even more pernicious than the inter-service variety. Army aviators fought for scarce funds and doctrinal status, finally concluding that only secession, the creation of a separate and independent Air Force, would free air power from its role as a supporting arm and permit it to reach its full potential, whatever that might be. Simultaneously, tank officers were sparring with the infantry for primacy as ground combat's essential "arm of decision." Naval aviators were squabbling with the battleship drivers for the same "arm of decision" designation, while few even listened courteously to the tinny reclamas of the submariners who would shortly prove so important.

These rivalries exploded and became institutionalized during World War II, often driving senior officers such as Army Chief of Staff George Marshall to despair. The diaries and memoirs of other leaders, civilian and military, reveal a similar exasperation. But there was no structure to control it. The Joint Chiefs of Staff evolved as an *ad hoc* body, with no statutory authority and scant resolve to say *No* to anybody. President Roosevelt's declared strategy was "Europe First." But to assuage inter-service rivalry (and to some extent popular opinion) he ended up dividing assets almost equally between Europe and the Pacific, then ran two separate Pacific wars: an Army campaign under General Douglas MacArthur and a Navy/Marine Corps effort under Admiral Chester Nimitz. Most distressing of all, there was no single civilian under the President who could adjudicate the squabbles and occasionally slap down a service or two. It was clearly understood that reorganization, although vital, would be so traumatizing that it had to wait until after victory.

That the war got run as well as it did must stand as a tribute to the character and intellect of the leadership, as well as to a considerable quantity of luck. Had the Battle of Midway gone to the Japanese, or the Normandy invasion been repelled, recriminations might well have torn the war effort apart. Victory becomes inevitable only in retrospect, and a working level of unity is easier to sustain when the news is good.

When the war ended, the United States had 12 million men and women on active duty. A year later, with only a million strewn around the planet and with funding to match, a nasty situation obtained. The smaller the force, the greater the internecine ugliness. At stake now was more than the rationing of postwar fiscal poverty. Each of the services was advancing its claims to Cold War roles, missions, and functions, and the money they generate.[9] Meanwhile, the Truman administration was crafting a new overall national security structure. Two years of vitriolic feuding produced the National Security Act of 1947. It was a mess.

In its military aspects (the Act also created the CIA and the National Security Council) the result was a structure artfully contrived to give the illusion of control while guaranteeing that the services and their internal branches would never be subject to effective discipline. The Act and subsequent legislation established a unified Department of Defense under a cabinet secretary. But there would be no "Minister of War" with extensive powers. The secretary was conceived as something akin to a college president—a kindly old gent, preferably an attorney lacking in military expertise, who would make speeches, hustle for bucks, and serenely broker such controversies as the Army, Navy, and Air Force secretaries (the "deans") couldn't settle themselves. The services retained the authority to write their own budgets and promote their own officers, subject to routine review but only rare major modification. America may have the most powerful military on earth, but the secretary of defense, by design, enjoys less power *vis-à-vis* his own department than many other cabinet members.

The Joint Chiefs of Staff finally gained statutory existence, but with serious practical limitations. The members, with the exceptions of the chairman and vice chairman, are also the uniformed heads of their services, and as such are expected and required to protect service interests. The tradition quickly arose that any advice given to civilian leaders would be based on "consensus," i.e., lowest common denominator. Not until the Goldwater-Nichols Department of Defense Reorganization Act of 1986 was the chairman even designated the President's principal uniformed adviser. An additional arrangement foregone: During World War II, Roosevelt had a "personal chief of staff" in the White House. The military determined that never again would the president have an in-house senior military adviser, independent of his service and able to offer unbiased and confidential counsel.

---

9. The terms "roles," "missions," and "functions" are often used interchangeably. They're not. Imagine the military as a theater company. Its mission is to stage *Hamlet*. For this it needs actors who play roles, plus a variety of supporting functions, from stage props to ticket sales. Each of these requires resources, so the competition for missions, roles, and functions is also a competition for budgets.

Further, there would be no "Prussian-style General Staff"—a separate body of officers who made their careers within that staff and could therefore function independent of service interests. Officers would come from their services for duty on the "Joint Staff," sometimes with explicit orders to protect their service's interests at all costs, and always with the knowledge that when their tour ended, they'd be going home: either to their service, or to retirement.

And this is the structure that, with some significant improvements in the realm of "jointness"—Pentagonese for a system in which every service gets a piece of the action—obtains to this day. It is utterly unsuited for the needs of the twenty-first century. As Marine General Anthony Zinni (now Secretary of State Colin Powell's special adviser and envoy on the Israeli-Palestinian conflict) put it during his 2000 retirement address at the U.S. Naval Institute:

> It [the 1947 Act] created a situation in which the biggest rival of any U.S. armed service is not a foreign adversary but another of its sister U.S. services. . . . We teach our ensigns and second lieutenants to recognize that sister service as the enemy. It wants our money; it wants our force structure; it wants our recruits. So we rope each other into a system where we fight each other for money, programs, and weapon systems.[10]

Those who think that General Zinni exaggerates might ponder a story told by retired Navy Admiral Bill Owens. In 1990, Owens commanded the Sixth Fleet in the Mediterranean, for decades a U.S./Soviet naval flash point. As the Soviet military collapsed, they pulled their submarines out of those waters; intelligence reported (correctly) that the boats were gone for good. Admiral Owens, himself a submariner, decided that the Sixth Fleet could now cut its own submarine presence from four to two.

"Within a day or two," he recounts in *Lifting the Fog of War*, "I received a ferocious telephone call from a three-star colleague in the Pentagon.

"*'How dare you?'* he accused me. *'If you don't support us, our opponents will take advantage and use this to cut the force!'*" (Italics in the original.)[11]

---

10. General Anthony Zinni, "Address at the U.S. Naval Institute, *Proceedings of the U.S. Naval Institute*, July 2000, Early Bird.
11. Admiral Bill Owens with Ed Offley, *Lifting the Fog of War* (New York: Farrar Straus & Giroux, 2000), p. 9.

Inter-service rivalry, then, is a defense fact of life engendered by technology, money, and organizational arrangements as well as by warrior pride. It cannot be underestimated or ignored. Even in times of great and genuine co-operation, it's always just beneath the surface. Consider the Army's barely concealed grumbling when the Marines went into Afghanistan first (Commandos don't count, only large units). As one journalist, Katherine Peters, noted: "The Army is either unable or unwilling to do its job. That's the message some mid-grade officers are getting from the deployment of hundreds of Marines to landlocked Afghanistan this week." Ms. Peters even quoted a noted Army officer and writer by name: "'It's a big slap in the face,'" said Maj. Don Vandergriff, an armor officer who teaches military science at Georgetown University."[12] (Internet traffic monitored by this author didn't put it quite so politely.)

Inter-service rivalry is also a fact of life for another reason. Historically, most world powers have disposed of far less force than they needed to handle their affairs comfortably. Power costs. Constant juggling and husbanding of resources have been the rule. Those who fret that America has grown soft because of our aversion to casualties might consider imperial Rome's stubborn unwillingness to shed unnecessary Roman blood. But America's twentieth century shortfall proved both unique and uniquely handled.

The Plans/Reality Mismatch

Irony can be pretty ironic. Although America disposes of more military might than any nation on earth, never have our resources matched our stated goals or adequately supported our declared strategies. Too often, the services and the Pentagon have enunciated utterly unrealistic objectives, for the purpose of justifying the maximum Congress would allot to defense and then squeezing out some more. German Chancellor Otto von Bismarck (Or was it Mark Twain? Or both?) once quipped that God protects drunks, fools, and the United States of America.[13] Militarily, this has been the rule more often than not. But in the Wars of the Ways, the fantasies so routine throughout the twentieth century no longer avail.

---

12. Katherine McIntire Peters, "Marine Deployment Irks Soldiers," *Government Executive*, 30 November 2001, Early Bird.

Since World War I, fantasy has reigned supreme. Two factors let America elide disaster in 1917–1918. There were two convoy routes to Europe: one for troops, one for supplies. The Germans, not overly impressed with American fighting prowess (a bad mistake later repeated by Herr Hitler), concentrated their submarines against the supply ships, thereby letting the entire American Expeditionary Force come ashore unchallenged. What might 20,000 or more American casualties at sea have done to American resolve in a war where, it turned out, support was three thousand miles wide and a few inches deep? Also, General Pershing demanded that American troops be kept under American command, not parcelled out to the British and French as cannon fodder, and allowed to train for months in quiet sectors. As a result, America took European-style sustained heavy casualties only for a few weeks in the spring of 1918, and during the final offensive that fall. In October 1918, the German General Staff, fearing communist insurrection at home, panicked. Had they chosen to conduct a fighting retreat, the war could have gone on many months more. In the War to End All Wars—hard to believe—America was barely tested.

In World War II, this country raised only about half the forces originally deemed necessary, and by 1945 was running out of draftable manpower: a fact usually ignored by those unwilling to understand why Hiroshima and Nagasaki were necessary. Part of the problem was an idiotically wasteful policy that rejected all those medically unfit for combat, without even considering alternative uses (a practice that continued through Vietnam). One result of this policy was that any invasion of Japan would have been mounted with troops who'd already fought their way across Europe, as well as with the surviving remnants of the Pacific campaigns. The Korean War demonstrated that America was hard-pressed to handle one minor conflict on the Asian peninsula, let alone defend Europe against the Soviet Union. NATO's 1951 Lisbon Conference, convened while the United States was still reeling from the Chinese onslaught in Korea, determined that there was no way the alliance could raise even a fraction

13. My boss, Ambassador Bruce Chapman, informs me that Bismarck said it and that the exact quote is: "God has a special providence for fools, drunks, and the United State of America." I do not dispute this, but am utterly convinced that so did Mark Twain. However, I have been unable to locate his quote. If anybody out there knows of a Twain version, please contact us. There's a couple of martinis riding on this.

of the necessary conventional forces to deal with what the Soviet Union might throw their way.

The American solution was a magnificent exercise in evasion. *De facto*, we'd rely on first use of battlefield nuclear weapons (in the most densely populated sectors of Europe) while pretending to field an adequate conventional force.[14] And yet, this bizarre theoretical reliance on nuclear weapons, as well as strategic deterrence, may be judged humane. Absent nuclear weapons, the West and the Soviet Union would almost certainly have come to blows.

Still, the charade went on. 1960s planning posited "two and a half" simultaneous conventional wars: one against the Warsaw Pact, one against China, and a "half war" somewhere. The half war that did materialize, Vietnam, nearly gutted the military for a decade. When Nixon opened China, the planners dropped one major war, reducing conventional requirements from the delusional to the merely preposterous. Jimmy Carter played with a "Swing" strategy, wherein American forces would win one war somewhere, then "swing" to the next. Ronald Reagan had more sense than to waste time on such constructs.[15] Desert Storm, another "half war," demonstrated once again that even little conflicts have a habit of consuming prodigious resources.

All of which is to say: When the Bush (senior) administration had to "size" its post-Cold War forces, it fell heir to the old tandem of *Pretend and Spend*.

The downsizing process actually began in 1990, when Defense Secretary Dick Cheney and General Colin Powell, then Chairman of the JCS, presided over the *Base Force Study* (*BFS*). Both men wanted a hedge against a renascent Soviet or Russian threat, which meant a force that could be quickly "reconstituted" to its previous inadequate level. And General Powell was adamant that, in order to avoid outright rebellion, cuts had to be apportioned evenly among the services. They concluded that the 1980s structure could be cut about 25 percent. In order to prevent further reductions at the hands of a Congress under pressure to produce something resembling a "peace dividend," they came up with an additional justification. The United States,

---

14. "First use" of battlefield nukes was not the same as "first strike," an attack on the USSR itself. Presumably, nuclear war could be confined to times and places of our choosing. To quote a great American philosopher: Sheesh.

15. With one exception: Navy Secretary John Lehman's "Maritime Strategy," to be discussed in Chapter 3.

AGAINST ALL TERRORS

according to the *BFS*, had to be able to fight "two simultaneous Major Regional Conflicts" (MRCs), one in Korea, the other in the Persian Gulf. Then came Desert Storm, an MRC which consumed most of our easily deployable active units, especially in Europe. Then came the subsequent and all-too-familiar postwar dismantling of the victorious forces.

And then came President Clinton, who turned a 25 percent reduction into a 40 percent reduction. From 1989 to 1999, the Army dropped from 18 active divisions to ten; the Navy from 566 ships to 317; the Air Force from 25 tactical fighter wings to 13.[16] Meanwhile Clinton sent the military on nearly 50 separate overseas missions, from bombing Iraq and Kosovo to policing Bosnia and humanitarian operations in Africa. In the fifteen years preceding the Clinton administration, a much larger force did only 20 such operations.

Officially, the military embraced the sudden primacy of MOOTW—Military Operations Other Than War. Unofficially, they seethed. They also didn't appreciate the lack of additional appropriations to pay for it. And what became known as the "Defense Death Spiral" set in. At first, the Pentagon used budgeted operations money to pay the MOOTW bills. Then they dipped into maintenance accounts. Then they started shifting money from procurement and R&D (Research & Development). In Pentagonese, the military experienced the "recurring migration of funds."

Meanwhile, the equipment was aging, with no replacements in sight. Planes designed and produced in the sixties and seventies were now expected to fly well into the twenty-first century. The Air Force opened an "Office of Aging Aircraft" and announced that it would operate its remaining 1950s-era B-52s until they were over *seventy* years old. Asked about this at a Congressional hearing, one Air Force general replied: "We're going to learn a lot about metal fatigue." The Army and Marines started looking at block obsolescence of vehicles purchased during the Reagan years. Naval vessels originally designed for thirty years of service were now reprogrammed for decades more. As everyone knows, older equipment (your car, for example) costs more to operate and maintain than newer models. Cannibalization and endless rebuilding of worn-out systems set in. Maintenance people found themselves taking parts (authorized or not) from one plane

---

16. Congressional Research Service, *Budgeting for Defense: Maintaining Today's Forces* (Washington, DC: GPO, 2000), p. ix.

or tank to keep another working. In many cases, parts weren't available at any price. The producers had either gone out of business or stopped dealing with the government—the "Vanishing Vendor Syndrome."

And thus the Defense Death Spiral: more work, less money, too much maintenance, too much deferred maintenance, too much self-cannibalization, too little innovation, and inevitably, too many good and promising young people getting out in disgust . . . or not coming in at all. Personnel costs also contributed to the Death Spiral. The Armed Forces are no longer composed primarily of young unmarried males, living in barracks and chowing down in mess halls (in PC Pentagonese, dining in dining facilities). It's an older, married-with-children force, which runs up the tab for housing, medical care, etc. Today, the Defense Department operates the world's largest single system of day care centers. Then there's the problem of keeping military pay at least marginally competitive with civilian opportunities, and all those exorbitant re-enlistment bonuses offered for critical specialties. Plus hundreds of millions for recruiting, and on and on.

How did the Clinton administration deal with this self-inflicted crisis? By a series of official studies and reports, all concluding that nothing *really* was wrong, except that there were some "challenges" that could be met by "initiatives" and, failing that, by spin and deft phraseology. First came the 1993 *Bottom-Up Review* (*BUR*) which, after a brief flirtation with a 2 MRC strategy called "Win-Hold-Win" (actually a throwback to the discredited Carter Swing) opted for confronting reality with word games. "Two simultaneous MRCs" became "two nearly simultaneous MRCs." Two years later, the *Report of the Commission on Roles and Missions* (*CORM*) also decided that everything was pretty much the way it should be. Two years after that, the 1997 *Quadrennial Defense Review* (*QDR*), a Congressionally-mandated self-study and master planning document, discreetly suggested that two nearly simultaneous MRCs might not be doable. So they changed MRC to MTW (Major Theater War) and "nearly simultaneous" to "overlapping time frames." And so it went, in study after study, report after report (the Defense Department submits about 400 reports annually to Congress alone). I'm OK. You're OK. We're all OK.

No-K. The Clinton administration's willful and sustained refusal to acknowledge the effects of its own policies made a bad situation worse, and threatened national security. In one sense, the Defense Death Spiral was inevitable, no matter who presided over it. At some point, aging forces have to be replaced, usually with more expensive equipment. All those upgrades and "retrofits" to existing gear also cost. But even this might have been manageable, had it not been for the great technological advances of the latter twentieth century. The real crunch came when it was realized that, courtesy of an accelerating process known as the Revolution in Military Affairs (RMA), the force couldn't just be modernized along prior technological lines. It had to be transformed. And it had to be transformed to deal with challenges beyond the conventional—known as "asymmetrical warfare" and "homeland defense"—as well as more familiar threats.

RMA

There are some mistakes so ridiculous that only experts can make them. In 1946, only months after Hiroshima and Nagasaki, Yale political scientist Bernard Brodie came out with a slender volume entitled, *The Absolute Weapon*.[17] Absolute as in final, ultimate, everything's been invented. In truth, nukes have proven neither ultimate nor all that useful as weaponry. And in a certain sense, the nuclear era represented not so much a radical departure as the culmination of a millennium-old trend toward larger and larger explosions, useful only because the accuracy of available delivery vehicles was so poor.

Bernard Brodie's "absolute" assertion—and his equally curious notion that the mission of the military was now to prevent wars, not win them—enjoyed several decades of pious invocation. But not everybody bought it. Among the dissenters was one of those wondrous mad Hungarian *émigré* scientists who worked so brilliantly in the 1940s and later on the defenses of their adopted country. John von Neumann argued, apparently with anybody who would listen, that there were two military revolutions going on: the nuclear and what he called the "computational." The latter, he predicted, would ultimately prove the more important.

He got it right. Gradually, computers improved the accuracy of missiles to the point where nuclear warhead yields could drop from

---

17. See Bernard Brodie et al, *The Absolute Weapon: Atomic Power and World Order* (New York: Harcourt Brace, 1946).

megatons to kilotons. Then as computers became ever smaller, cheaper, and more available, and more and more stuff got computerized, it began to seem that the very nature of war might be changing. The Soviets may have noticed this first. They called it the "Military-Technological Revolution." By the latter seventies, their military journals were filling with assessments, and their minds with foreboding that their tottering semi-Industrial Age economy couldn't keep up.[18] Around the same time, a few Americans took notice. The term that stuck: Revolution in Military Affairs, or RMA.

It's hard to tell when the American RMA began. Admiral Owens picks 1977, when "three key Pentagon officials—Harold Brown, Andrew Marshall, and William J. Perry—began to think in concert about the application of technology to military affairs."[19] It's an attractive date. The RMA, then, began just as the military was sliding toward its worst years under President Carter. And Andrew Marshall, since those lean years head of the Pentagon's internal "think tank," the Office of Net Assessment, was chosen by Donald Rumsfeld to preside over his own 2001 comprehensive defense review. Even at the Pentagon, perseverance can pay off.

In its initial phase, the RMA entailed the application of microprocessor technologies to military affairs, with its first real test courtesy of Saddam Hussein. The Gulf War proved a strange event. It was in some ways an Industrial Age climacteric, the last of the great armor campaigns, fought in the sand against Iraq instead of on the plains of central Europe against the Warsaw Pact. But it also provided the merest first glimpse of what an RMA force could do. All that gee-whiz gadgetry—those laser-guided bombs ringing bunker doorbells; those cruise missiles stopping for red lights in downtown Baghdad; not to

---

18. Since the end of the Cold War, it has become clear that there was indeed a dangerous, out-of-control Military-Industrial Complex. But it belonged to the USSR, and may have consumed 30 percent of Soviet peacetime Gross Domestic Product. By the mid-eighties, they'd amassed an utterly unsustainable conventional force, including 50,000 tanks of all shapes, sizes, and states of repair. The prospect of the block obsolescence of most of the Soviet military terrified the leadership. One of the reasons the Strategic Defense Initiative (erroneously aka "Star Wars") so worried the Soviets was not their belief it would ever work well enough for the United States to launch a nuclear strike. It was fear that they might have to divert exceedingly scarce technical resources to developing counter-measures, at a time when the economy was approaching collapse.

19. Owens, *Fog*, p. 81.

AGAINST ALL TERRORS

mention real-time intelligence gathering, GPS navigation, superb communications—made America seem, well, invincible.

The aura of invincibility lingered, even as the Death Spiral set in. Simultaneously, the services took off wildly in all directions, exploring the possibilities of transformation and the appropriations they might engender.

The Army decided to "digitize the battlefield" via "sensor to shooter real-time awareness," generating hypothetical constructs with the ease of moving a mouse. "Force XXI" segued into "The Army after Next," and "The Army after Next" into "The Army after Next and a Half." By decade's end, there were Legacy Forces, Interim Forces, Objective Forces. There was the Future Combat System of vehicles, actually a hypothetical network-centric something-or-other. There was the Land Warrior Program for developing near-term RoboGrunts, not to mention Future Warrior 2025, an "integrated uniform" that would "weigh no more than 15 percent of a soldier's body weight and consist of six major subsystems: headgear, combat uniform, physiological monitoring, microclimate conditioning, weapon and power supply."[20] Meanwhile, the Army demanded a few score billions for "recapitalization" of existing forces and warned that all this novel gadgetry may actually require more people—officers, especially—to operate and manage.

The Navy also got into the game, touting "network-centric warfare" and dallying with such novel concepts as the "Arsenal Ship," a heavily armed barge of sorts. There was also the "Street Fighter." Odd name for a ship, but then its proponents touted it as more fighter plane than boat, boasting that it would feature crew "ejection seats" for emergencies.[21] Then there was SEA LANCE, an acronym standing for "Seaborne Expeditionary Assets for Littoral Access Necessary in Contested Environments." The Navy also warned that real transformation would take several decades, at least. A self-fulfilling prophecy, perhaps, as they steadily backed away from radical changes to their most important and expensive ships, and sought a few score billion extra to keep building replacement vessels along traditional, i.e., mid-twentieth century designs.

---

20. George I. Seffers, "U.S. Army Envisions New Kind of Soldier," *Defense News*, 14 February 2000, Early Bird.
21. "Admiral: Like Aircraft, 'Street Fighter' Will Feature Ejection Seats," *Inside the Navy*, 9 July 2001, p. 1.

Two other services, the Air Force and Marines, exhibited more measured enthusiasm. The former spoke happily of "virtual presence" and "effects-based operations," of "global strike" and "global strike task forces." But they also understood that the RMA pointed inexorably toward unmanned aircraft and toward space: a troublesome challenge to their pilot-dominated culture. Meanwhile, the Marines got into the game by hanging computers on lance corporals, who complained that they could no longer shoot straight because of the chest harnesses. They also ramped up their interest in urban warfare, a battlefield where technological superiority often proves useless, and in developing and using a variety of non-lethal weapons. These now come in endless real and proposed models, from Sticky Foam (an aqueous gel that hardens into an immobilizing Styrofoam-like solid when sprayed on crowds) to a polymer spray that works like a sheet of ice, sending rioters and other evil-doers slip-sliding away. Not to mention ultra-sound and microwave weapons that function like phasers set on stun.

Ten years into the exercise, as might be expected, there have been a lot of failures and dry holes, as well as some promising developments. But it's been slow, far too slow. And unfortunately (or perhaps fortunately), while the military has struggled with RMA Phase One, the action has moved on. RMA Phase Two continues the exploitation of computers, but also enters exotic new areas, especially robotics, nanotechnologies, MEMS (Micro-Electro-Mechanical Systems), and weaponry such as lasers and particle beams. In a sense, RMA Phase One was about doing things the military has always done, only far better and faster. Phase Two enters the realm of the hitherto (except in sci-fi) unimaginable . . . against enemies also hitherto unimaginable.

Why so slow? Why has the military barely gotten into Phase One when Phase Two's already aborning? Many reasons may be adduced, from justifiable skepticism and conservatism to perennial lack of funds. But whatever the reasons, and no matter how valid, they confirm a single fact. The RMA is not inevitable. Transformation won't happen on its own. The new technologies must be developed far more rapidly. And in fact, something of the sort started in the weeks after 9/11. Any number of must-have research projects were advanced, and Pentagon "solicitations for proposals" concerning various technologies flew off the fax machines daily. By one estimate, the Defense Department probably received 20,000 counter-terrorism proposals from the private sector in three months.[22] From quick ways to decontaminate anthrax-infested buildings to hand-held devices that can sense infrared emissions from Afghan caves, the momentum of change is accelerating. But it must be institutionalized.

Of course, no technological advance yields a revolution unless it gets applied in the real world. And no revolutionary application works unless it generates corresponding changes in the structure and operations of the organizations, and in the minds and habits of the people who work them. American business figured this out in the eighties and nineties. Work forces got downsized, bureaucracies flattened, new techniques and perspectives adopted. During this same period, the military struggled merely to appliqué the new technologies onto existing organizations, with predictable lack of success. True to the spirit of the Wasted Nineties, they camouflaged the charade by issuing endless transformational "Vision Statements." If they ran short on details, they ran long on touchy-feely, reaching perhaps new heights of depths with "The magnificence of our moments" in one Army statement.[23]

How far did the services go during the Wasted Nineties to avoid following the RMA to its logical structural and organizational conclusions? *De facto*, they made it their primary mission to play with the technologies while evading their implications. They did it constantly, in every venue from high-level official studies to joint staff exercises, from war planning and resource allocation to doctrinal publications. Admiral Owens, who ended his career as Vice Chairman of the Joint Chiefs and perhaps the most prominent RMA advocate, writes: "I have been very sad to see resistance and outright bureaucratic opposition toward the RMA at the highest levels of the defense establishment."[24] If nothing else, the opposition revalidated the old adage (attributed to B. H. Liddell Hart) that the only thing harder than getting a new idea into the military mind is getting an old one out. One particularly egregious example may stand for thousands here. This one goes by the name of "Halt."

---

22. See Susan Carpenter, "Pentagon to Public: Any Bright Ideas?" *Los Angeles Times*, 2 November 2001, Early Bird. Also see "Officials: DOD Could Receive Up to 20,000 Counter-Terrorism Proposals," *Aerospace Daily*, 30 November 2001, Early Bird.
23. Available at www.army.mil. Look under "Past Statements."
24. Owens, *Fog*, p. 18.

Halt

The problem began, as usual, with the airplane. Or more aptly, with the pilots. By the 1920s, it was clear that air power had become a permanent part of war. But how to use it? Traditionalists saw the airplane as merely an extension of other supporting arms and functions, different in form and capabilities but not in use. Airplanes could bomb and strafe; that made them flying artillery and machine guns. Airplanes could reconnoiter; that made them airborne cavalry patrols. Airplanes could transport; that made them flying trains or cars or mules.

Air power advocates demurred. The airplane, they prophesied, could prove decisive in war, if only it were unshackled from the restraints (physical and mental) of the land and sea services. The problem was, their premise was hard to prove in peacetime, especially when funds were scarce and already spoken-for, and public interest minimal. And so, with the most honest and noble of intentions, air power advocates set out on a fifty year campaign of overpromising, overselling, and generally getting on everybody else's nerves.

In World War II, strategic bombing of enemy cities killed millions and obliterated cities, but failed to produce anything resembling decisive—let alone cheap and fast—results. It did produce horrific losses. Statistically, a man stood a slightly better chance of surviving in an infantry unit than in a bomber crew. Aircraft were throwaway items. The Army, Navy, and Marines remembered all the good things that didn't quite happen. And they took special umbrage at postwar Air Force assertions that, well, maybe the Combined Bomber Offensive of World War II didn't quite deliver, but just give us jets and missiles and a few thousand nukes and you guys can go play golf. Neither Korea nor Vietnam did much to bolster the Air Force claim to primacy. To put it mildly, the Army was not always happy with the quality of support they received from an Air Force seemingly more concerned about Navy competition than battlefield success.

Still, after Vietnam, as a vastly-outnumbered and outgunned Army pondered how to deal with a possible Warsaw Pact invasion of Europe, they reached a startling conclusion: *"The Army cannot win the land battle without the Air Force."* This statement, taken from the 1976 edition of the Army's basic field manual, *FM 100-5* and italicized in the original, announced the advent of a happy time between the Army and the Air Force. The result of this sudden new appreciation was the Army's *AirLand* doctrine of the 1980s, which held that the Warsaw Pact could be defeated (*sic?*) by a synchronized set of air strikes deep behind the enemy's front forces. Synchronized, that is, with the Army's ground war. Appreciation stopped well short of equality, or of any concession to the notion of an independent and decisive air campaign.[25]

Then came Desert Storm and a stunning air war, conceived by a small coterie of brilliant officers. Granted, Saddam Hussein proved an astonishingly co-operative enemy. Nonetheless, air power had done nearly everything its early advocates had promised. It had crippled the enemy's homeland. It had isolated the battlefield, making Iraqi reinforcement and resupply impossible. It had pounded enemy forces into an punch-drunk stupor and had obviated the need for a prolonged, bloody ground campaign. No, it hadn't made war antiseptic. No one claimed that it had, or ever would. But it had demonstrated that, after half a century's worth of hyperbole and disillusionment, the RMA had shown that air and space power could deliver.

And then, as the lessons of Desert Storm were studied and the force and budget reductions implemented, the Air Force began to wonder if maybe a change in American strategic and operational doctrine might be in order. The five year fury that wonderment sparked became known as the "Halt Phase Debate."

The premise of "Halt" was far from implausible. It made no claims to sole or automatic "arm of decision" status. It never argued that air power alone could bring victory, and never suggested that ground forces were now unnecessary. It did hold that the military needed to consider a new option. American strategy since World War II had been to let the bad guys strike first, stabilize the situation, concentrate forces, then attack. Under this scheme, the "culminating point" was the counter-offensive, chasing the enemy back to Berlin or the Yalu River or Moscow or Baghdad or wherever. The bulk of resources, naturally, went to the ground forces. Air power's job was to help halt the enemy offensive, help stabilize the front, run "deep interdiction" missions behind enemy lines, maybe pummel their

---

25. See Rebecca Grant, "Deep Strife—The Legacy of 1980s AirLand," *Air Force Magazine*, June 2001, Early Bird.

homeland a bit, until the ground forces got their act together. Air power would then support the land campaign.

Desert Storm suggested that it might be otherwise. In fact, perhaps the real "culminating point" of the war should be the "Halt" phase, not the counter-offensive phase. After all, once the enemy had been stopped, he'd effectively lost. The United States would then have time for a leisurely buildup and, given the intensity of air bombardment, might not require a massive, costly land campaign at all.

The other services replied, forget the Gulf War. After all, endless Pentagon simulations consistently showed "Halt" to be impossible anywhere else. As retired Air Force General Chuck Link tells the story, he noticed that TacWar, the then-standard computer war game, always showed airpower's effectiveness dropping drastically after the first few days of conflict—the reverse of the Desert Storm experience. He requested a briefing on TacWar. He was informed by his briefer that the model assumed the Air Force would run out of munitions. General Link responded that it was possible to buy and store munitions. The briefer then noted another reason why air power's effectiveness declined. After the enemy was halted, they retreated to "deep underground bunkers" which, presumably, they'd either brought with them or were somehow able to construct while under fire. General Link:

"I was curious, so I asked, 'Deep underground bunkers: what goes on in there? do they train in there? is there enough room to drive tanks around? how much food is there? do you suppose their health improves during that time?' Finally, I asked, 'When they come out, can we still kill them?'"[26]

The Air Force never claimed, despite endless Army claims that they did, that air power could guarantee a quick and tidy victory every time. The Air Force did argue that an early and decisive halt meant that we'd have time for a more thorough mobilization and buildup. One might think the Army would appreciate this. In fact, the exact opposite obtained. Buying more Air Force planes and munitions meant less money for the Army. And more time for mobilization meant more time to bring in the National Guard and reserves as major combat (not merely supporting) units. From the Army perspec-

---

26. Center for Strategic and International Studies, *Clashes of Visions: Sizing and Shaping Our Forces in a Fiscally Constrained Environment* (Washington, DC: CSIS, 1997), p. 19.

tive, it was bad enough to propose that air power could replace "boots on the ground" to any significant degree. But to suggest that "Halt" also empowered the "weekend warriors" . . .[27]

The debate flared and sputtered for several years, then re-emerged in 2001. After much mastication, the Air Force had succeeded in getting the "Halt" notion inserted into *JP 3-0*, the primary joint doctrine manual, as a possible option. Then Army General Henry Shelton, Chairman of the Joint Chiefs of Staff, excised any and all official mention—although there is some verbiage about "seizing the initiative" that the Air Force considered an OK elision.

(And then came Operation Enduring Freedom, and the use of precision air power to shatter a government, take out caves, etc., and now the debate over the air power/land power relationships flares again.)

The Wasted Nineties witnessed endless "Halt" debates, large and small. As the decade ended, a new contretemps, this time Navy versus Air Force, this time on "Access," began to emerge. How best to assure that American forces could get ashore and remain operational and well-supplied, given possible enemy use of WMD to destroy or block access to critical ports, airfields, and transportation systems? These spats could get vitriolic and tempestuous, yet they were, by and large, conducted within the framework of the traditional inter-service understanding: business-as-usual lest, once the changes begin, they cannot be contained. But even as business-as-usual proceeded, even as any number of good ideas from all quarters went nowhere, people were starting to notice new kinds of threats. And some were starting to draw an unpleasant conclusion concerning the relationship between those emerging threats and the ability of the nation to provide for the common defense.

Asymmetries

Desert Storm was fought against a conventional force that used conventional Soviet weapons and operated along the general lines of Soviet doctrine. China, North Korea, and a few other potential enemies also field more or less conventional forces. None can stand up to

---

27. The literature on the "Halt" debate is voluminous. For two good examples, see Center for Strategic and International Studies, *Clashes of Visions, op cit.,* and Rebecca Grant, *Airpower and the Total Force: The Gift of Time* (Washington, DC: IRIS Independent Research, 1998).

an RMA force whose "system of systems" is functioning smoothly. Therefore in all probability, none will ever try.

After the Soviet collapse, American planners decided that no "peer competitor" was likely to emerge for several decades. A more plausible scenario involved a "regional near peer competitor," capable of some pretty hefty combat in his own little corner of the world. But if no conceivable conventional force could match an RMA force, and everybody knew it, how might these "near peers" choose to fight?

The answer: asymmetrically.

The concept of asymmetrical warfare became perhaps the most popular military buzzword of the Wasted Nineties. In its simplest sense, it means anybody who doesn't stand up and fight fair, i.e., the way you want them to fight. This is, of course, no new thing. Asymmetrical warfare has always been the weapon of the weak against the strong. Endless examples come to mind, especially the classic guerrilla versus regular forces match-up. But three aspects of modern asymmetrical warfare accentuate the potential power of the weak.

An RMA force offers enormous opportunities for enemies to develop "niche capabilities" that can do significant damage. For example, in a 1994 Naval War College game set around 2015, China savaged the U.S. Seventh Fleet without ever putting a hull of their own in the water. They did it with land-based anti-ship missiles and an anti-satellite capability that knocked vital communications and intelligence assets out of business faster than we could replace them. Cyberwar offers another splendid example of asymmetry. Don't attack the force, attack the computers that hold it together.

Another novelty involves WMD, the "Revenge of the Melians" factor. For practical purposes, the United States is out of the WMD business. We're destroying our stocks of chemical weapons. We're prohibited by Act of Congress from developing any new nuclear warheads, although there's occasional talk of developing "micro-mini nukes" for use against chemical and biological weapons and stockpiles. The advantage, presumably, is that nuclear temperatures would vaporize the baleful agents, not release them.[28] But lots of other folks are getting into WMD big-time, either by purchase, indigenous development, or some combination of the two. These weapons provide

---

28. See H. Josef Hebert, "Officials Back Low-Yield Nuclear Strike against Bioweapon Stockpiles," AP Release, 19 December 2001.

AGAINST ALL TERRORS

dandy niche capabilities for relatively weak forces, especially in their "anti-access" and "area denial" usages. Chemical and radiological weapons can be used to contaminate vital seaports, airports, storage depots, and other facilities permanently, or just long enough.

But perhaps the most chilling new form of asymmetric warfare involves such weapons in the hands of non-state actors . . . and the possibility that they might use them against the American homeland. Never before in history have small groups been able to possess such power. As 9/11 showed, these weapons don't always come in traditional forms. As Tom Ridge, Director of the Office of Homeland Security, aptly noted, an airplane crashing into a building becomes a weapon of mass destruction. An envelope containing anthrax has the potential to become a weapon of mass death.

Throughout the Wasted Nineties, some officers, some analysts, some writers saw it coming. Over and over, they pointed out that an RMA force had to be able to do more than defeat a non-RMA force in "fair," i.e., Desert Storm-style combat. An RMA force had to be able to cope with asymmetrical warfare in all its forms. Some even asserted that, face it, *we're the asymmetry*, and we'd better understand how uniquely vulnerable that makes us. If the "system of systems" goes down, upon what do we rely? And toward the end of the decade, a new phrase entered—or, more precisely, re-entered—the military lexicon.

Homeland Defense

The 1997 *Quadrennial Defense Review* had little to say on the matter, noting only that "[W]hile we are dramatically safer than during the Cold War, the U.S. homeland is not free from external threat."[29] It listed homeland defense as a "priority"—Beltwayspeak for "No serious action will be taken." But Congress, sensing that the *QDR* would be a whitewash, had chartered a "National Defense Panel" to present an alternative view. Their December 1997 report, *Transforming Defense: National Security in the Twenty-First Century,* laid it out, and is worth quoting at length:

> Protecting the territory of the United States and its citizens from 'all enemies both foreign and domestic' is the principal task of gov-

---

29. *Report of the Quadrennial Defense Review*, May 1997, Section II, p. 2, at www.defenselink.mil.

ernment. The primary reason for the increased emphasis on home-land defense is the change, both in type and degree, in the threats to the United States. . . .

Threats to the United States have been magnified by the prolif-eration of, and the means to produce and deliver, weapons of mass destruction. . . . The complexity of the WMD challenge lies in the number of potential enemies who have access to, and may choose, this asymmetric means of attacking the United States in an effort to offset our conventional strengths.[30]

Three years later, yet another group was chartered to provide alternatives to yet another *QDR*. The "U.S. Commission on National Security/Twenty-First Century" (sometimes also known as the "National Security Study Group") looked at the progress of homeland defense and found little. Despite a flurry of Clinton initiatives, bureaucratic game-playing, and ramped-up federal spending ($10 bil-lion or so in 2000, depending on how measured), there was still no serious effort, and only a somewhat increased emphasis on "conse-quence management."

Worse than apathy was bureaucratic chaos. Over forty separate federal agencies, fifty states, and uncounted local authorities were involved. The Secretary of Defense had a new special assistant for "civil response" and the new Norfolk-based Joint Forces Command had some sort of responsibility for the military aspects of conse-quence management. The services were fielding small threat detec-tion units, mostly for their own use. The National Guard had launched an ill-fated attempt to establish several dozen RAID (Rapid Assess-ment and Initial Detection) units. After three years, none had been certified operational. Military trainers, working under the auspices of the Nunn-Lugar-Domenici Act of 1994 had "visited" dozens of cities to offer their expertise and gear to local police and fire departments. But in reality, little had been accomplished beyond the rudimentary, the cosmetic, and the pointless. Often, the visitors merely antago-nized the local "first responders" by their arrogant "We're from Washington and we'll tell you how to do your jobs" demeanor. Actual defense of the homeland was still, as they say within the Belt-way, a "non-starter."

---

30. National Defense Panel, *Transforming Defense: National Security in the Twenty-First Century*, at www.defenselink.mil.

AGAINST ALL TERRORS

And so, in *Road Map for National Security: Imperative for Change*, the Commission called for the creation of an independent National Homeland Security Agency and urged the new administration to "calmly prepare the American people" for what lay ahead.[31]

Sometimes you'd rather not be right.

---

31. See The United States Commission on National Security/Twenty-First Century, *Road Map for National Security: Imperative for Change*, Chapter 1. The Commission had also highlighted this danger in its first report, *New World Coming*, issued in 1999. All are available at www.nssg.gov.

3

This People's Next Defense

On September 10th, 2001, Donald Rumsfeld was one of the most picked-on, abused, and discounted men in Washington, DC. Three months later, he was everybody's favorite "minister of war" and even the normally rational *National Review* took up opining on his status as media god and sex symbol: "What's more, with every appearance, some say, he's making additional conquests, not of Herat this time, but of hearts, the hearts of women all over America, each beating a little harder at the thought of a man who, these ladies like to believe, doesn't need the help of a B-52 to make the earth move. . . . Chicks dig chiefs . . ."[1]

Well, OK. But the issue here is Donald Rumsfeld before the media decided it was cool to be Donald Rumsfeld. His effort to think through transformation before attempting it had earned him six months of growing military and Congressional enmity, and media reports with headlines like "The Secretary Bombs, Again" and "Rumsfeld's Lonely, Losing Battle."[2] *The Weekly Standard* was calling for his resignation for failure to spend money fast enough. There were even Pentagon betting pools, offering odds on how long before he resigned. And if he stayed, everyone knew (or hoped) that the October 1st release of the *Quadrennial Defense Review* would kick off the most virulent Pentagon slugfest in fifty years. It would be Rumsfeld against a Military-Industrial-Congressional Empire that (as Pontius Pilate told Jesus in *The Last Temptation of Christ*) did not want things changed. Not even for the better.

The Quadrennial Defense Review (*QDR*) came out on schedule, to mild surprise and a massive display of indifference. The conventional wisdom held that, due to the changed nature of the world, transformation would go on indefinite hold, and that defense spending would "draw a bye" for at least one year. Business-as-usual, pork as usual, and everybody's pet projects get a reprieve. The *QDR*, a pre-9/11 matter, was DOA. And Donald Rumsfeld, according to the wisdom *du jour*, "will be judged on prosecuting the war instead of on transforming the Pentagon bureaucracy."[3]

---

1. Andrew Stuttaford, "Rummy and Juliet: Adonis Rumsfeld," *National Review Online*, 12 December 2001, Early Bird.
2. William M. Arkin, "The Secretary Bombs, Again," *Washington Post*, 13 July 2001, Early Bird; Frank Pellegrini, "Defense: Rumsfeld's Lonely, Losing Battle," *Time*, 9 August 2001, Early Bird.
3. Mark Mazetti and Richard J. Newman, "Rumsfeld's Way," *U.S. News and World Report*, 17 December 2001, Early Bird.

Once again, the conventional wisdom got it wrong.

QDR

On October 1st, 2001, the Department of Defense released one of the most astonishing documents in American military history. The responses of the defense community and media were equally astonishing. Nobody noticed or, if they did, found nothing of note. Some, including a few of our more ferocious legislators, even dismissed it as verbal pabulum, an evasion of the hard choices, not worth the effort of the download, etc. Business-as-usual also includes clichés as usual.

They could not have been more wrong. That is, assuming that words have meanings, and that document said what it meant, meant what it said, and that the opposition within the Pentagon and the Congress could be overcome. Among the indicators that Mr. Rumsfeld was serious—he found the time to put aside his duties as a media icon of virility long enough to establish somewhere around fifty new panels to get to work on the hard choices; he established a Pentagon Office of Transformation; and he named a leading advocate, retired Admiral Arthur Cebrowski, to head it.

Recall, please, what the *2001 Quadrennial Defense Review* was supposed to do—at least from the Congressional, think tank, and media perspectives. The *QDR* is an official self-study that sets forth (along with the defense secretary's annual *Report to the President and the Congress* and several thousand other documents) the department's goals, priorities, and strategies.[4] When Donald Rumsfeld came back to town, the 2001 *QDR* process had been underway for nearly a year. For six months, his *ad hoc* study groups completely overshadowed the *QDR*. Senior officers considered it wasted effort at best, and didn't mind saying so. In the summer of 2001, the *QDR* rather unexpectedly revived. Nobody, however, was sure what it would produce. Would it codify Mr. Rumsfeld's decisions regarding what would get transformed and what would get cut? Or would it signal, in some way or other, some sort of military revolt? (Although the *QDR* is "owned" by the Office of the Secretary of Defense, it's mostly a product of the Joint Chiefs of Staff.)

---

4. As a rule, the length of any defense document is inversely proportional to the size of the force it describes, i.e., the smaller the force, the greater the verbiage. In traditional military parlance, this is known as the "Words to Weapons" or "Tooth to Tongue" ratio.

AGAINST ALL TERRORS

In either case, the *QDR* was the balloon that was supposed to hit the fan.

9/11 shredded all assumptions. Suddenly, nobody knew what was necessary, except that everything was now necessary, and now was no time to make changes. Arguments over fiscal restraint, also overtaken by events. The Congressional cash machine went into hyperdrive. So naturally the *QDR* couldn't make the hard decisions. Those had to go on hold until the situation started to sort itself out.

Much of the *QDR*, especially regarding transformation, is vague. Much of the rest is standard Pentagon boilerplate, especially the traditional forlorn verbiage about reforming accounting and procurement procedures. But in six vital areas, the *QDR* completely reverses American strategic and operational doctrine.

That is, assuming words have meaning. Given Mr. Rumsfeld's performance to date, it's a reasonable assumption, even if he did get a bit over-folksy (part of the charm?) at a December 2001 press conference. "There are some who say that when you're in a war, by golly, it's not time to do anything else. I don't agree with that. I think that, by golly, we have to go forward with transformation."[5]

By golly.

First, the *QDR* returns homeland defense to its rightful status as "the foundation of strategy." Gone are the centuries of nearly total invulnerability to attack, when America was shielded by broad oceans and blessed with non-aggressive, if not always beatific neighbors. Gone also are the decades of total vulnerability to Soviet nuclear attack, enshrined in the aptly named doctrine of MAD (Mutual Assured Destruction). Gone also is the last century's notion that America's "real" borders run through central Europe, along some tier of "friendly" Middle Eastern states, thence to some sort of Asian/Pacific line. In short, we may be the most powerful nation on earth, but we've also re-entered the ranks of the most ordinary. We can get hit. We have been hit. "Therefore," according to the *QDR*, "the defense strategy restores the emphasis once placed on defending the United States and its land, sea, air, and space approaches. . . . Protecting the American homeland from attack is the foremost responsibility

---

5. Jonathan Weisman, "A Warrior in One Battle, Manager in Another," *USA Today*, 21 December 2001, Early Bird.

of the U.S. Armed Forces and a primary mission for the Reserve Components."[6]

In truth, however, the quote misspeaks a bit. Homeland defense entails far more than merely "restoring the emphasis" from an era of coastal forts, or even of jet interceptors. The principle of homeland defense as the primary responsibility of government may be permanent. But the complexity of this effort will be utterly unprecedented.

Second, the *QDR* shifts "the basis of defense planning from a 'threat-based' model that has dominated thinking in the past to a 'capabilities-based' model for the future. This capabilities-based model focuses more on how an adversary might fight, rather than whom that adversary might be or where a war might occur. It recognizes that it is not enough to plan for large conventional wars in distant theaters. Instead, the United States must identify the capabilities required to deter and defeat adversaries who will rely on surprise, deception, and asymmetric warfare to achieve their objectives."[7]

This can only be described as revolutionary. In the past, most conventional forces were deemed "general purpose," available for duty anywhere doing anything. The Army assumed that if their forces could handle the most demanding contingency, large-scale, high-intensity mechanized warfare in Europe, everything else (such as chasing Viet Cong guerrillas or Somali warlords) would fall into place. The Navy and Air Force made similar assumptions in their own realms. No more. Now the fundamental issue will be: What do we need across the entire spectrum of peril, not—What will it take to deal with the North Koreans or the Iraqis?

Third, the *QDR* sketches new synergies between forward-deployed forces tied to specific places, most notably Europe, Japan, and Korea, and long-range capabilities based in the United States, capable of rapid deployment and employment anywhere:

> New combinations of immediately employable forward-stationed and deployed forces; globally available reconnaissance, strike, and command and control assets; and information operations capabilities; and rapidly deployable, highly lethal and sustainable forces that may come from outside a theater of operations . . .[8]

---

6. *Quadrennial Defense Review,* 30 September 2001, pp. 14, 30, at www.defenselink.mil.
7. Ibid, p. iv.
8. Ibid, p. 25.

The implications here are enormous, and enormously liberating. If done correctly, there will be a quantum increase of effectiveness, due to an axiom as fundamental as the *systems proliferate/effects converge* principle. (See the Appendix for General Principles of Transformation.)

A force that is smaller and more specialized, yet also more easily transported, deployed, and sustained, is far more versatile than a bulky, ponderous "general purpose" force tied to specific theaters and contingencies. Axiom time again.

In the twenty-first century, versatility is a function of specialization plus mobility.

Or, to use a civilian example, which is the more efficient and profitable: a home repair company that has twenty specialists (carpenters, plumbers, electricians) each with a fully equipped van, or fifty handymen who share a few all-purpose trucks?

Fourth, the *QDR* commits to comprehensive transformation in a rational manner, devoid of the technological intoxication that sometimes leads to over-promising and under-achieving. "Of necessity," the document states, "our efforts will begin relatively small, but will grow significantly in pace and intensity. And over time, the full promise of transformation will be realized as we divest ourselves of legacy forces and they move off the stage and resources move into new concepts, capabilities, and organizations . . ."[9]

That's a genteel and diplomatic statement, reflecting the world of last September. Since then, Mr. Rumsfeld has suggested more than once that it's time to pick up the pace. The President has supported him, and even the Congress is urging him on.[10]

Fifth, the *QDR* aims toward a new level of inter-service co-operation, by evolving joint forces from the current "everybody gets a slice" approach to forces that are "task-organized into modular units," run by Standing Joint Task Force Headquarters. These would then be made available to the CINCs, the regional commanders-in-chief, who until now have drawn their forces directly from the services. Not to

---

9. Ibid, p. v.
10. Donald H. Rumsfeld, "Beyond This War on Terrorism," *Washington Post*, 1 November 2001, p. A-35. See also Paul Mann, "Bush Urged to Accelerate Military's Transformation," *Aviation Week and Space Technology*, 3 December 2001, Early Bird.

stretch the analogy too much, it's the difference between dining *a la carte* and ordering the dinner special.

Time also, the *QDR* hints, to develop a more flexible operational doctrine. Traditionally in joint operations, everybody supports, or is supposed to support, or ends up supporting the Army. Not all the furor of the "Halt" debate could change that fact of doctrinal life, and the new "Access" debate—how best to assure that American forces can get ashore anywhere, anytime—seems to revive the notion that everybody's prime duty is to support the land war. On the surface, yes. But now there may be times when the Army should support the Air Force, the Air Force support the Navy, etc. And in truth, this is no new thing. During World War II, for example, the Marines "supported" the Army by taking Saipan, Tinian, and Iwo Jima for their use as bomber and fighter bases. In the 1973 Yom Kippur War, Israel crossed the Suez Canal to take out the Egyptian surface-to-air missile batteries that were hampering air operations. In effect, the Army "supported" the Air Force.

Finally, the *QDR* points toward a new and long overdue aggressiveness in the conduct of operations. The MRC/MTW paradigm remains. But the goal is now to "[s]wiftly defeat aggression in overlapping major conflicts while preserving for the President the option to call for a decisive victory in one of these conflicts—*including the possibility of regime change or occupation . . .*"[11] (Italics added)

Remember Desert Storm stopping short of destroying the élite Republican Guard and the subsequent failure to oust Saddam Hussein? Remember the Korean War and a stalemate that festers to this day? Remember the years when U.S. declaratory strategy toward a Warsaw Pact invasion of Europe was to "restore the border on favorable terms"? Remember Vietnam?

Remember the Taliban?

No longer should a real or potential enemy assume that his regime's existence will not be threatened, or that it cannot be terminated. Nor can foes expect to enjoy future sanctuaries: "Combat operations will be structured to eliminate enemy offensive capability across the depth of its territory."[12] This may include the combat capabilities of subnational and transnational groups resident in those states. The Afghan campaign has established the precedent.

---

11. Ibid, p. 17.
12. Ibid, p. 21.

In sum, a magnificent paradigm that gets its priorities straight, shows a new comprehension of how to make war, and pushes toward a revolutionary new force based upon new technologies and new organizations. However, to borrow from the poet Robert Burns, "There's many a slip 'twixt the zipper and the zip." Can it be done?

The answer is a definite maybe, provided it can be done without igniting the Pentagon civil war that always seems just about to happen. One way to do this is offered herein. To explain, it's necessary to take a look at what it is that the Army, Navy, Air Force, and Marines actually do . . . and how they've adapted since the end of the Cold War. Then we offer a new way of thinking about these services and their various "core competencies" and "operational arts." We call it "Space Force, Peace Force, Warriors, Guard." It's not a reorganization proposal, just an alternative view. After the events of the last century and the last few months, such a view may have value. Finally, some thoughts on the possible renascence of the citizen-soldiery via and yet another principle of transformation, one still not clearly discerned.

Twenty-first century technologies, as well as twenty-first century perils, empower eighteenth century virtues.

But first, while we're on the subject of virtue, two brief statements concerning those who wear the uniform today, and will wear it tomorrow. For ultimately it's human beings, not technologies and organizations, who fight.

It is true that in time of war the dangers and sufferings fall more heavily on the young than on their elder leaders. But it is also true that their seniors, the current flag officers and colonels especially, merit attention. For they are those who did not get out during the Wasted Nineties, when frustration levels were catatonic and civilian career opportunities plentiful. They constituted themselves as a saving remnant of America's military, and are worthy of respect and gratitude for it.

This is not the first time. The great leaders of World War II endured the indifference of the twenties and the privations of the thirties. In the seventies, a few thousand officers did the rethinking that made the Reagan rearmament possible, and that gave the world Desert Storm. The Wasted Nineties, as we shall see, were far from entirely wasted. Tens of thousands of good men and women held to their posts. They've emerged as architects and executors of a brilliant campaign, and are now ready to emerge as effective creators of transformation. They're worthy custodians of the young lives placed in their charge.

So far, no mention has been made so far of the cultural aspect of the Wasted Nineties—the Clinton era deluge of scandals and pseudo-scandals and forced changes regarding women, homosexuals, sensitivity training, relaxation of standards, and the rest. The initial version of this book dealt with these subjects at length, both the depredations in all their ugliness, and the ugliness of some of the opposition to them. But I have chosen to forego these issues here for one overwhelming reason. That was then. This is now.

We're at war. And war, not theories or preconceived notions of any kind, will show whether those policies and efforts and the changes they wrought were wise. History will judge. Until then, every man and woman in uniform needs and deserves nothing less than unconditional respect and support.

Army, Navy, Air Force, Marines

So what exactly do these people do? At first, the answer seems obvious. The Army fights on land. The Navy does water. The Air Force tends to the wild blue yonder and beyonder. The Marines sail around on ships, hit the beaches, and provide PRMs for the other services.[13] And all the services organize, equip, and train forces for the regional unified commands outside the United States, and now for possible use within the country.[14]

But of course and naturally, it's never as simple as that. The Army maintains its own air force (mostly helicopters) and its own Space Command, and has been designated the operator of whatever national missile defense system might get built someday. Indeed, the Army's influence in space is growing. In October 2000, an Army officer, Lt. General Edward Anderson, became deputy commander of the U.S. Space Command. In November 2001, another Army officer, Brig. General Stephen Ferrell, became the Defense Department's "national security space architect."

---

13. Positive Role Models.
14. There are five regional unified commands: European; Central for the Middle East, Gulf, and central Asia; Pacific; Southern for Latin America; and Joint Forces for the United States. The Pentagon has indicated that it's giving serious consideration to establishing a Northern Command for homeland defense.

The Navy deploys both its own air force (carriers) and its own army (the Marines, who also have their own air force), plus a Space Command of its own. The Air Force, which was designated in May 2001 the principal service for space (which may explain the growing Army presence), spends much of its time supporting its sister services, despite all the palaver about taking large chunks of their jobs. All the services maintain special operations and unconventional warfare capabilities. The Marines, traditionally the most inward-looking of the services, now provide more and more senior officers for high-viz joint command and staff assignments And everybody's moving into counter-terrorism and homeland defense, albeit with a wary eye toward spending too much money on it or letting it interfere with more cherished activities and concerns.

However, despite all the overlaps and rivalries and the implications of the *systems proliferate/effects converge* principle discussed earlier, the services still remain the "Keepers of the Art" in their respective "core competencies." Army: sustained large-scale land combat, limited but growing fast-response emergency forces (paratroops, etc.). Navy: fleet action, power projection, sea lane protection, support of land operations. Air Force: short and long-range air power, airlift, space. Marines: forcible entry from the sea, forward deployed units available for emergency duties, capability to organize for large-unit sustained combat ashore when necessary.

Taken together, these core competencies provide a force utterly unique on this planet. Numerically, the American military is not nearly as large as it seems, only about 1.4 million on active duty, another million-plus in the reserves. But it generates power several orders of magnitude above all other forces. No other nation maintains a fleet of large deck aircraft carriers and a Marine Corps larger than many nations' armies. No other nation builds stealth bombers or Abrams tanks, unarguably and by far the finest ever. Since the collapse of the Soviet Union, no other nation has even dreamed of matching American submarines, military satellites, airlift. None can.

So they don't even try. The peril of "asymmetrical warfare" has already been addressed. So has all the good stuff contained in the *QDR*. Now the question becomes: What are the services doing to deal with these threats, while simultaneously maintaining and enhancing their ability to prevail in more traditional forms of combat? The answers show once again that the Wasted Nineties were far from entirely wasted. But before getting into each service, there are two more axioms that must guide the exercise.

As a rule, conventional military forces come in two general kinds: territorial and expeditionary. A territorial force fights in and around where it is. It's usually designed to address known and predictable threats, and is therefore somewhat limited in its range of capabilities. The Israel Defense Force provides a perfect example; so does the Swiss militia. Both are excellent for their purposes. Neither will wake up tomorrow with orders to head for some other continent.

An expeditionary force, by contrast, goes somewhere else to fight, often a very far away somewhere else. Expeditionary forces must be structured so that they can travel and be sustained at long distances. Often, expeditionary forces do not know where and against whom they might operate. Their range of capabilities must be greater.

American forces are and shall remain primarily expeditionary. Homeland defense does not mean creating forces to fight on American soil.

But these are expeditionary forces of a unique kind. The United States is neither a land nor a sea power, as these terms have traditionally been used. We are no nineteenth or twentieth century Germany or Russia, our interests best protected and advanced by massive armies. In fact, these powers got themselves into a great deal of trouble when they tried to develop world-class navies. They antagonized those who needed the sea far more than they did and forced some very costly and ultimately pointless arms races. Nor are we a Carthage or a British Empire or an Imperial Japan, dependent on sea power for our very existence. We need both, obviously. Expeditionary forces must be balanced.

However, we are in essence an aerospace power, the first and so far the only such. And we're just beginning to explore the meanings and potential of that status. Aerospace is the great American advantage. It must never be lost or endangered, and always advanced.

Aerospace does not mean exclusively Air Force.[15] It means the combined capabilities of the services, from Army helicopters to Air Force B-2 bombers, from cruise missiles to satellites. And although aerospace power may not be relevant to every situation, Afghanistan shows that it grows more relevant all the time. Without all those networks of air and space-based surveillance, reconnaissance, and communications, precision warfare and what's known in the trade as

RDO (Rapid Decisive Operations) become impossible. As a general rule, whatever can be done from the air and space, should be done from the air and space.

Expeditionary. Aerospace. These guide the future. Now let's look at each of the services, as they struggle to make their great power relevant.

Army

The United States Army came out of Vietnam shattered in body and spirit. Then, courtesy of a saving remnant of brilliant and dedicated officers, it revived and rebuilt, first intellectually, then physically. The fall of the Soviet Union left it without a Goliath to face. Desert Storm redeemed it . . . despite the primacy of air power, and perhaps a little too well. When air power can decimate anything that moves, when ground armored combat "exchange ratios" exceed ten to one, when the Abrams tank ranges the battlefield at will, taking target practice on enemy vehicles from "stand-off distances" (you can reach them but they can't reach you), why do you still need massed tank and mechanized infantry divisions?

You don't. As one gentleman involved in Persian Gulf planning told me some years ago, they could handle Saddam's twenty-first century army with five armored brigades of a few thousand men each, not five divisions totaling a hundred thousand or more. They knew they could. But to admit it would be to justify further cuts to an Army whose strength dropped by half during the nineties.[16]

But inventory shrinkage has been only one of the dilemmas. America's Army is, almost by definition, expeditionary. But for fifty

---

15. The term "aerospace," although commonly accepted, is actually a misnomer. True, the "aero" realm shades gradually into the "space" realm. But operating in the two is totally different. Air operations typically last hours; space operations, from a few days (the shuttle) to many years. Air operations depend on complex ground-based supply and support systems. Space operations such as satellites must take everything with them, or depend on extremely expensive and difficult repair and resupply via space shuttle. Finally, air operations depend on humans in the cockpit . . . although this is changing as UAVs (Unmanned or Uninhabited Air Vehicles) and UCAVs (Uninhabited Combat Air Vehicles) are developed and fielded. Space operations depend on robotic or remotely controlled machines . . . although this is changing as the human presence in space grows.

16. See also Eliot A. Cohen, "Iraq Can't Resist Us," *Wall Street Journal*, 18 December 2001, Early Bird.

years the Army maintained a *de facto* territorial defense force in Europe: large formations garrisoned where they would fight, with an extensive network of supporting bases and other organizations. They'd created a smaller version in Korea, and for ten years in Vietnam. They'd also evolved intricate, sometimes ridiculously ambitious plans for rapid reinforcement in Europe and elsewhere: flying troops in from the United States to draw weapons and equipment prepositioned in warehouses or afloat.

In retrospect, it was astonishing to what lengths the Pentagon would go to deal with the Plans/Reality Mismatch. One of the most ambitious—some might say ludicrous—reinforcement schemes of the Cold War was the so-called "Ten/Ten Plan"—ten divisions good-to-go against the Soviets in Europe within ten days of alert. Six of these divisions were to fly in, draw their POMCUS (Prepositioned Organizational Material Configured in Unit Sets) gear, and head for their positions on the line—with the Soviets busily bombing, contaminating, or otherwise disrupting every seaport, air field, and railhead they could (the old access dilemma). And also while the civilian population clogged the highways. However, NATO doctrine regarding civilians called for them to stay home and watch the war on TV, so maybe it wouldn't have been so bad.

By the nineties, the need for the European garrison was waning, and the possibilities of creating a similar structure in the Persian Gulf were virtually nil, due to host country reticence. This meant that most remaining Army forces would be based within the United States, and would have to be able to deploy quickly. But armored units and mechanized infantry (troops travelling in their own armored vehicles, nowadays the M-2 Bradley) are heavy, difficult to transport, and a monstrous challenge to sustain. The Army would have to "lighten up"—in more ways than one—while retaining firepower sufficient to overwhelm any foe.

In practical terms, this meant three things, none of them exceptionally palatable to the traditionalists. The Age of the Tank, with its heavy armor, chemically-fired guns, and endless thirst for fuel was over. The M-1 Abrams is the last heavy tank the United States will ever build. The Abrams, despite its troubled development—all major weapons have "troubled" developments—turned into a masterpiece. One of the greatest ironies of the Gulf War was that all the systems that performed so well, from the M-16 rifle to the Abrams tank and most of the aircraft, had "troubled" developments: cost overruns, scandals, etc. But the weapon that gets fixed isn't news.

The heavy tank, it was now clear, really had utility only in wide open, relatively flat spaces. At eighty to ninety tons, it was too heavy to cross half the bridges in western Europe, let alone maneuver in Third World urban sprawls or chase guerrillas or terrorists. Further, the thing had simply gotten too complex. Studies after Desert Storm suggested that even the better crews could only work it at about sixty percent efficiency. The tank was approaching the complexity level of the airplane.

If the Army's favorite weapon was now magnificently obsolete, so was its favorite organization. Divisions come in all shapes and sizes, but with the exception of the 82nd Airborne, they have one thing in common. They're essentially mini-armies, combining many types of weaponry and support functions, capable of extended operations (paratroops generally don't operate as divisions for long periods). They range in size from 12,000 to 20,000 or more, when reinforced with various capabilities. And they're obsolete.

The divisional structure, with its rigid hierarchies and specialized staffs, actually predates the Industrial Revolution; Napoleon would be right at home. It was designed for an era when armies moved slowly, communications were rudimentary, and supply trains ponderous. Today, the exact opposite prevails. The heavy division has to go, and the Army has known it for decades.

Still, there's a nasty problem to be faced before the traditional divisional structure can be retired, or at least reduced to a purely administrative status. All the services have the problem, but it affects the Army most severely.

The military, unlike virtually any other large modern organization (except the Catholic Church), cannot draw its midlevel and senior leadership from outside its ranks. Your generals today were your lieutenants three or four decades ago: no exceptions. Moreover, the military has no real way of knowing how many generals will be needed in thirty years, or how many colonels in ten, or even how many lieutenants in five. World War II demonstrated that we could turn out a basic lieutenant, a "Ninety Day Wonder," in about six months. We were also able, not without pain, to find the right senior leadership. The problem was the middle—an explosion of demand for colonels and junior generals, officers who required many years of training and experience to fit their duties.

After World War II, the Army concluded that the next war would be like the last, a long affair requiring major mobilization. So it decided, in effect, to "stockpile" excess peacetime officers on active duty against that future need. But what to do with these guys? The inevitable bureaucratic answers: grade creep, bloated staffs, make-work assignments, endless schooling.

Abolition or even serious reform of the divisional structure would eliminate a lot of already scarce, and highly prized, command and staff jobs.[17] No bureaucracy gives up its midlevel employment base willingly.

Finally, the Army had to face the perennial access problem. Europe and Korea at least had forces on the ground. In some future conflict, they might not even be able to get ashore. Air and sea port facilities, highways, and prepositioned equipment, might be contaminated by chemical, biological, and radiological attacks from enemy governments or other groups. Thus, the Army had to create units that were lethal on whatever battlefield might beckon; easily transportable for inter-continental distances; and capable of setting up for business without the accustomed infrastructure.

Or to put it somewhat differently, the Army needed to become more like the Marines while increasing its dependence on the Navy and Air Force, a need demonstrated by its failure to deploy effectively to Kosovo as well as by the pre-eminence of the Marines in Afghanistan.

For most of the decade, the Army diddled with a variety of games and gizmos. Then, in October 1999, General Eric Shinseki, the Army's chief of staff, laid out a remarkable vision for Army "transformation." He divided the Army into three conceptual structures: the present "Legacy Force," a near-term "Interim Force," and a transformed "Objective Force" a decade or two out. To get the process rolling seriously, he called for new kinds of rapidly deployable Interim Brigade Combat Teams (IBCTs) of several thousand soldiers, capable of building into any kind of force needed. His goal: a brigade anywhere in the world within 96 hours, a division on the ground anywhere in 120 hours, five divisions anywhere in 30 days. That avail-

---

17. A counter-argument holds that new types of organization might actually require more officers, given the requirement for around-the-clock operations.

AGAINST ALL TERRORS

able air and sealift could never sustain such movement was less important. The impetus was to create new kinds of units that could be tailored into new kinds of divisions or light corps.[18]

General Shinseki also demanded serious consideration of abandoning heavy tracked vehicles (tanks and infantry carriers) and moving toward a lighter, all-wheeled force. Exotic new types of weaponry, as well as improved versions of older equipment, would be required. Rifles and machine guns ye have always with you. But how about equipping every grunt with insect-sized disposable flying sensors? Combat vehicles, also always. But how about a fifteen-ton vehicle with revolutionary new lightweight armor and an electromagnetic rail gun that shoots hypervelocity kinetic energy rounds? How about a "distributed tank," its move/shoot/communicate functions spread among several vehicles? The possibilities converge in something called the Future Combat System, or FCS, which the Army regards as the absolute *sine qua non* of its transformation. They're still not very sure what it is, but they have to have it.[19]

The work's underway at various Army centers, amid the inevitable griping and resistance. At the moment, it's too early to tell whether the new IBCTs, the FCS, and other hypotheticals, will produce a genuine technological and operational revolution, or whether they'll end up as a Worst of Both Worlds travesty—too heavy to transport, too light to fight. The first IBCTs are supposed to be operational by 2004, but may come on-line earlier. General Shinseki wants a serious "Objective Force Capability" fielded by 2010, probably earlier, without waiting for full testing and development of all the hardware and software. At the moment, the approach seems less irresponsible than daring. A post-9/11 report by the General Accounting Office (Congress' investigative arm) considers the plan high-risk but "well-crafted" and capable of responding to future events.[20] As Dan Gouré, a respected Beltway defense analyst, sums it:

> Creating the Objective Force will be a wrenching experience for a Service used to thinking in terms of combined-arms operations based on integrated, but nonetheless distinct, branches. Creating the

18. Eric K. Shinseki and Louis Caldera, "The Army Vision Statement," 1999, at www.army.mil.

19. "FCS Will be 'Cornerstone' of Transformed Army, Bolton Tells SASC," *Aerospace Daily*, 5 December 2001, Early Bird.

20. "GAO: Well-Crafted Army Transformation Plan Faces Many Challenges," *Inside the Army*, 19 November 2001, Early Bird.

Future Combat System may require something more: a scientific miracle. . . .

The FCS is truly a leap into the unknown. It is not a weapons platform, like a tank or APC [armored personnel carrier]. It is envisioned as a network-centric system of systems centered on a common vehicle platform. . . . FCS depends on multiple, parallel revolutions in science and technology achieved at a pace unknown in peacetime.[21]

Which was exactly how the Manhattan Project, creator of the first atomic bomb, went about its business.

Then there's the vexatious problem of which units to specialize for the new struggles and how. The Army currently maintains, in addition to armored forces, mechanized infantry, heavy infantry, light infantry, mountain infantry, airborne infantry, air assault infantry, and myriad other specialties. Merely creating one new type of conventional force would not reap the benefits of exploiting the *systems proliferate/effects converge* and *specialization plus global mobility means versatility* axioms. Transformation may not involve every unit in the Army, but it should be carried through the whole spectrum of capabilities in some form.

And finally, there's the matter of what to do with the parts of the Legacy Force that must be good-to-go tomorrow. At the moment, the Army wants to "recapitalize" segments of the present structure to create a chunk of the "Interim Force"—upgraded tanks, the new (but still traditionally designed) Crusader artillery piece, and a number of other so-called "legacy weapons," originally designed for Cold War scenarios. The bill for it all will be, even by post 9/11 standards, mega.

It's far too early to tell whether the Army can achieve a genuine transformation that would make it quickly deployable, devastatingly lethal, and sustainable against myriad threats. Perhaps the best, or least bad, of all possible worlds would be the construction of a *de facto* three-tiered Army. One segment would be thoroughly transformed, one would remain a modestly recapitalized interim force for less demanding missions, and one would be designated for peacekeeping/peace-enforcing duties, and structured and trained accordingly.

---

21. Daniel Gouré, "Transformation: Will It Fix What Ails the Army?" *Armed Forces Journal International*, October 2001, Early Bird.

AGAINST ALL TERRORS

Navy

The Navy's act of statesmanship came nearly a decade ago. So far, its transformation has not matched its vision. The 600-ship Navy planned by Ronald Reagan (they got up to about 585) now numbers less than 325. If present trends continue, the active fleet will fall to about 286 ships by 2007. Current aircraft purchase requirements run about two hundred per year. 122 are budgeted; by one account the Navy intends to buy only 81 in FY 2003.[22] Clearly, the Navy has been in a Death Spiral of its own, more and more money going into fewer and fewer platforms that may or may not be relevant to the new threats. And no matter how capable any ship, it can only sail one sea at a time. Size may or may not matter. Numbers matter.

Fortunately, there is a solution. What the Navy must do now is meld its statesmanship of the nineties to the logic of transformation. They may not end up with a fleet they like, perhaps not with anything that even resembles a traditional fleet. But the shift away from an aircraft carrier-based to a submarine-based force (multi-mission attack subs, not the ballistic missile-toting "boomers"), with a new emphasis on smaller vessels of great versatility, will be reality sooner or later. Preferably, sooner.

By tradition, culture, and desire, the Navy has always been the most independent of the services. "The United States Navy will neither confirm nor deny that it belongs to the Department of Defense"—so muttered many an exasperated general, civilian official, and reporter over the last half century. Some muttered far worse.

In part, this independence derived from the old, i.e., pre-radio days, when the ship's captain wielded unique and uniquely independent powers, both over his crew and the actions that his vessel might take. It also derived from the service's "complete-unto-itself-ness." As already noted, the Navy comprises far more than ships. It operates its own air force (carriers), its own army (the Marines), and its own nuclear deterrent (missile-firing submarines). It also doesn't need the other services, certainly not in the ways the other services need them, for transportation and other forms of support. Finally, for over a century, the Navy had defined its primary mission as fleet action on the

---

22. David Brown and Amy Svitak, "Analysts: Navy Purchase Plans Reduce Capabilities," *Defense News*, 29 October 2001, Early Bird. See also "Navy Gives Rumsfeld FY-03 Budget," *Inside the Navy*, 3 December 2001, Early Bird.

high seas, i.e., taking on other navies. This might involve World War II-style naval combat, or other missions such as protecting sea lanes, or seizing islands or coastal real estate. Whatever the task, the same characterization of the fleet prevailed.

"It's big. It's gray. It goes away."

After World War II, this fixation on fleet action slowly ceased to correspond with reality. There was no foreign navy out there to fight, at least not in the pre-1945 manner of carriers and surface ships against carriers and surface ships. The Soviet Navy was a submarine-based force. Its ventures into surface warfare (large cruisers, small aircraft carriers, naval infantry), although well-publicized, proved decidedly unimpressive, and were ended by the collapse of the USSR.

Still, tradition and budget justification decreed a fleet action mission. Attempts to define such a mission against the USSR reached a ludicrous climax in the 1980s, with the publication of the so-called "Maritime Strategy." This doctrine, Navy Secretary John Lehman's creative approach to the naval aspects of the Plans/Reality Mismatch, held that in event of war with the USSR, the Atlantic Second Fleet would sail up to the heavily defended Kola Peninsula, launch carrier strikes against naval and air bases on Soviet soil, and maybe land the Marines to seize a facility or two. The Pacific Fifth and Seventh Fleets would bottle up the Soviets in Vladivostok. The Mediterranean Sixth Fleet would, presumably, seal off that sea and keep the Soviet Black Sea Squadron where it belonged. All this failing, perhaps we'd sink the Soviets in an old-fashioned high seas *melee*. All this while dealing with several hundred enemy submarines and supporting NATO ground and air operations in Europe.

No one ever identified a single sailor or Marine even minimally eager to try.

The "Maritime Strategy" notwithstanding, ships—lots of ships— were still too useful to do without. The Reagan goal was a 600-ship fleet, based on fifteen carrier battle groups: aircraft carriers and a dozen or so escorting vessels. There would also be four surface action (battleship) groups; a hundred or so attack submarines; and several dozen amphibious assault ships for the Marines (vessels specially designed for amphibious combat operations, not mere troop and supply transports). Except for the subs, this was in reality a force more for projecting power ashore in regional hot spots and showing the flag (a fine nineteenth century euphemism for intimidating the locals) than for slugging it out with the Russians, either at sea or on Soviet soil.[23]

When the USSR dissolved, so did its navy; no branch of the Soviet military collapsed more completely.[24] There was no longer a fleet anywhere in the world even marginally capable of challenging the U.S. Navy. Nor would there be, despite a few desultory attempts to envision a Chinese naval threat-in-waiting. Air power advocates love to proclaim, "There's American air power and there's everybody else's." Naval proponents could now make the same claim, with equal justification. But what to do with the fleet tradition?

Wisely, the Navy chose to accept the demise. In 1992, the service issued a short paper, . . . *From the Sea*, then followed it with *Forward . . . from the Sea*. These papers announced "a change in focus, and therefore in priorities for the naval service away from operations on the sea toward power projection and the employment of naval forces from the sea to influence events in the littoral regions of the world—those areas adjacent to the oceans and seas that are within direct control of and vulnerable to the striking power of sea-based forces."[25] While still touting the Navy's unique capabilities across the spectrum of operations, from showing the flag (also known as presence missions) to possible minor fleet action against regional navies, the documents made it clear that the Navy was ready to surrender its centuries of total independence, more or less.

Since then, the Navy's *Maritime Concept* paper has laid out a reasonable set of organizing principles for the new century; in the fall of 2001, they got to work on a new "vision statement" that includes the naval aspects of homeland defense.[26] Unfortunately, the Navy has proven far less willing to change its fleet than to change that fleet's missions and operations. Once again, bureaucratic turf protection prevails. The service is composed of three major "communities"—naval

---

23. With, of course, the major exception of operations against Soviet subs.
24. Admiral Bill Owens, then commander of the U.S. Sixth Fleet in the Mediterranean, tells of signaling a Soviet captain to have a safe journey home. The man replied, "I no longer know where my home is." See Admiral Bill Owens with Ed Offley, *Lifting the Fog of War* (New York: Farrar, Straus & Giroux, 2000), pp. 68–9.
25. Department of the Navy, *Forward . . . from the Sea* (Washington, DC: GPO, 1994), cover letter.
26. Amy Svitak, "U.S. Navy's New Vision to Stress Homeland Security," *Defense News*, 3–9 December 2001, Early Bird.

aviation, submarines, surface warfare—and resources have generally been allocated evenly among them. The "platform barons," as the senior officers of each community are sometimes called, fear radical change even when it serves their own interests, so great is their aversion to the kind of internecine strife that, once started, might get out of hand. To his enormous credit, Admiral Bill Owens, when serving as a deputy chief of naval operations in the early nineties, took on the platform barons. Post-Cold War Navy cuts were not distributed in the classic "let's ration the poverty proportionately" manner. Submarines and surface vessels endured deep cuts; the aviation community, relatively few. At the time, it may have been a wise apportionment. It was certainly deemed necessary to protect naval aviation from the other services. With the demise of the Soviet Navy, surface ships and submarines could be cut more than proportionately. Unfortunately, long-term, we've got the wrong kinds and numbers of ships.

Reorienting and restructuring the fleet has proved no easy job. Nearly two years before . . . From the Sea, Desert Storm revealed the magnitude of the undertaking. No service fared worse in that endeavor. Naval aviation played second cockpit to the Air Force. It was primarily an Air Force show and, in any event, carriers generate far fewer sorties than land bases.[27] More embarrassing was the Navy's skittishness about operating in the restricted waters of the Gulf. When one ship hit a mine, the rest steamed off in a manner not seen since Admiral Fletcher abandoned the Marines at Guadalcanal.

Was the decision correct? Probably. Close-in naval forces, including a possible Marine landing in Kuwait, weren't needed to win the war. Still, the Navy had to spend much of the nineties explaining that . . . From the Sea didn't necessarily mean, "Close to the Beach." Certainly it didn't in an era of readily available mines, nasty shore-based anti-ship missiles, and quiet diesel subs that can lie on some littoral bottom, just waiting for opportune targets.

Two greater problems also got in the way of the Navy's good intentions. One was the shrinkage of the fleet. Naturally, the fewer the vessels, the more loath the Navy becomes to lose or even risk them. The other problem: long lead times. You don't change the composition of the fleet overnight, or even over a decade. The Navy has

---

27. One major problem was that the two services didn't have compatible communications. Air Force daily tasking orders had to be flown out to the carriers.

AGAINST ALL TERRORS

to adapt with what it's got left for "brown water" littoral operations while still maintaining its "blue water" open ocean capabilities.

Today, the Navy remains an aircraft carrier-centered force; it's still building large (100,000 ton) Nimitz-class nuclear-powered carriers and expects to operate a dozen for most of the twenty-first century.[28] Plans for radical carrier redesign have foundered on cost and risk. "CVNX-1"—the first carrier to evolve away from the Nimitz-class model, keeps getting less evolutionary and more expensive all the time. The Navy may not even begin work until 2007.[29]

Meanwhile, the carrier's worth grows ever more suspect, save under the most benign conditions: no threats, total freedom to operate and resupply. Granted, they're not that easy to sink or incapacitate. But they're too expensive, both to build and to operate. Nimitz-class carriers were designed in and for an era of cheap labor. Conscription meant that the Navy would always get enough real and "draft-induced" volunteers. A ship and air wing crew of five to six thousand is about two thousand too many. Further, three carriers are needed to keep one on-station anywhere: one deployed, one back from deployment in maintenance, one gearing up to head out. Then there's usually one laid up for extensive overhaul.

As the Afghan air campaign developed in the fall of 2001, the Navy began to sense a certain redemption. Most of the missions over Afghanistan were flown off carriers, which in the Navy mind demonstrated once again that carriers are essential when land bases are lacking. Yes, replied the Air Force, but most of the bombs were dropped by less than twenty Air Force long-range bombers, which don't require local bases. In addition, according to the Air Force, the global range and expeditionary restructuring of the Air Force (to be explained momentarily) vitiates the Navy's old "We Go Where the Air Force Can't" argument. Finally, cheaper alternatives such as Tomahawk cruise missiles, which can be launched from almost any ship, cut into the need for piloted aircraft, Navy or Air Force.

Both kinds of forces are needed, obviously. But the balance should change. The Navy must cut its carrier fleet from twelve to about nine, but should keep one or two of its older models and recon-

28. For a good *precis* of the carrier's future, see Bill Sweetman, "Naval Aviation Shows Force as Carrier Boom Continues," *Jane's Navy International*, June 2000.
29. "First CVNX Carrier May Slide a Year or More, Could Drive Up Cost," *Inside the Navy*, 29 Oct. 2001, Early Bird.

figure them as Marine and/or Army amphibious assault ships. This change has already happened, *de facto.* When the USS Kitty Hawk, one of three remaining oil-fired carriers, headed toward Afghanistan, it carried soldiers, not fighter planes. Also, aircraft carriers have spacious (by Navy standards) medical facilities and can be expanded into hospital ships of sorts. Given the perennial shortage of amphibious assault ships and the inevitable need for treating casualties, conversion makes both financial and military sense.

Surface combatants present a similar problem. Traditionally, frigates, destroyers, and cruisers were designed for blue-water duties such as defense of carriers and sea lane protection. They can be and have been adapted to littoral operations. Modular weapons systems and software packages can be tailored and installed. But often these are patches at best, and fail to provide what the ground forces (especially the Marines) would dearly love to have—ample naval gunfire and missile support for operations ashore. In fact, the ground forces consider the development of such support the true test of the Navy's commitment to operations ashore. Further, if the Navy wishes to counter enemy "anti-access" threats, it needs much longer-range and more accurate naval guns than it currently possesses.

So far, not much has happened by way of new ships designed for support of land campaigns. In recent years, a number of radical proposals have been (pardon the pun) floated. The Navy spent several years on the DD-21 Zumwalt-class "land attack destroyer," another endlessly troubled program. However, the DD-21 developed into a rather too-large vessel, over-missiled and under-gunned, not very likely to sail in close, or survive very long if it did. In November 2001, the Navy decided to scrap the DD-21 in favor of a modular "family of ships" known as "DD-X."[30] A good decision, if it works.

By now, it should be apparent that in some ways the Navy has the same problem as the Army—how to avoid building forces that are too bulky yet too small to fight, specialized yet versatile. No one believes that a few large platforms can meet global requirements. But no one wants to build a "PT Boat Navy" that can work the littorals, but has limited use on the high seas and falls into the "expendable" category.

The problem can be solved by a decent mix of large and small ships, coupled with increased reliance on submarines: ships with, at

---

30. Anne Marie Squeo, "Navy to Scrap New Destroyer Plans in Favor of Building 'Family of Ships,'" *Wall Street Journal*, 31 October 2001, Early Bird.

AGAINST ALL TERRORS

first glance, about as much utility for twenty-first century land operations as the horse cavalry (which proved remarkably useful during some of the Afghan ground engagements). Submarines have a tendency to surprise. Indeed, the entire history of the submarine is a tale of unpredicted and implausible adaptations.

Prior to the First World War, subs were regarded as defensive coastal weapons. The Germans demonstrated that submarines could operate with fierce effectiveness on the high seas, individually and in "wolf packs." The United States Navy took note, but even in World War II, it regarded subs as essentially "force multipliers"—relatively low-cost investments that paid fine dividends. But the "real" Navy was the big stuff, first battleships, then carriers.

In 1946, Hyman Rickover, then a going-nowhere Navy captain, recognized that nuclear propulsion would transform the submarine from a surface ship capable of limited undersea operations into a genuine high-endurance submersible. The Navy showed minimal interest. The real enemy, one admiral told Rickover, was the Air Force; nuclear-powered carriers came first. Capt. Rickover pointed out that if you could scale a reactor down to fit in a sub, scaling it up to fit in a carrier or cruiser would be easier. He got permission to try and, twenty years later, the "Silent Service" had evolved from a well-regarded curiosity to a separate fiefdom within the Navy. Attack submarines evolved to hunt other subs and surface ships. The "boomers," the large ballistic missile subs gave the Navy a nuclear deterrent force to rival the Air Force.

When the Soviet fleet disintegrated, it seemed that the attack boats had little left to do, save perhaps to chase Third World diesels or freighters hauling suspicious cargo. But it quickly became apparent that the submarine's inherent virtues of stealth and endurance, plus its ability to handle many kinds of missions, had enormous potential for the support of land operations. Intelligence-gathering, surveillance, and reconnaissance tasks, naturally: These missions had been routine during the Cold War. Now add to these many kinds of special operations, from landing SEALs and other élite forces to counter-terrorism and whatever else you might care to fantasize about. Finally, submarines make fine cruise missile launchers. Especially the Tridents, which could carry hundreds, if modified. Four Tridents are scheduled for decommissioning under treaty arrangements with Russia. Plans call for modifying two as cruise missile boats. All four should be so reconfigured.

At the moment, the attack sub fleet dwindles toward 50. A recent Pentagon study estimated that at least 65, more probably 75, are needed to meet intelligence-gathering and operational requirements laid on by the regional combatant commanders-in-chief.[31] As one admiral rather evocatively put it to me a few years ago: "This [the sub force] is not a self-licking ice cream cone."

In sum, the Navy recognized early on that it had to abandon its traditional independence and, to borrow a Biblical phrase, "bring forth fruits befitting repentance." Whether it can do so is still very much in question. To adapt another phrase: the spirit is willing, but the body's hard to reconfigure. Still, this country desperately needs a strong Navy, to wit, about 400–425 ships, including nine aircraft carriers, 75 or so attack subs, 150 evolving large surface combatants, 50 or so smaller ships for littoral operations, and several dozen amphibious assault ships for hauling Marines and—from time to time—soldiers.

Air Force

What do you do
When your dreams come true
And it's not quite like
You planned?

So sang the Eagles, a popular rock group of the 1970s. "After the Thrill Is Gone"—apt description for the eagles and others of the Air Force. Yes, the United States is uniquely an aerospace power. Yes, aerospace is and will remain our weapon of choice whenever possible. But for three reasons—two simple, one complex—the Air Force since Desert Storm has faced a cumulating set of challenges that amount to the greatest crisis in its history, a mix of challenges and dilemmas that, in some ways, the current Afghan success only worsens.

The first reason is, simply, the Wasted Nineties wore the Air Force out. You can't spend ten years boring holes in the sky over Iraq; you can't commit half your tactical fleet to Kosovo; you can't

---

31. Bradley Graham, "Pentagon Warns against Cutting Attack Sub Fleet," *Washington Post*, 4 January 2000, p. A-3.

fly your planes with pilots who aren't there, or fix them with technicians and chiefs who've gotten out, or with parts that are no longer available. Something has to give and, despite the adrenalin rush of the present season, something will give unless the Air Force gets a lot of cash, and fast.

Tactical aircraft are aging rapidly. Twenty years ago, it became common to joke that the B-52s were older than the crews who flew them. Now the same can be said of an increasing number of the fighters. The F-22, the first new fighter in four decades, may provide some relief if it ever goes into full production; initial production begins, hopefully, in 2002. But at $180 million a copy (roughly $62 billion for the program) it is far too expensive to procure in the needed quantities. Even the current full buy of 339 wouldn't meet global requirements. The Joint Strike Fighter, a multi-service, multi-national program, will be built by an international team headed by Lockheed Martin; the $200 billion initial contract was awarded in October 2001. But the first aircraft are several years away, at least. The intercontinental transport fleet, despite the new C-17, remains an unsteady mix of aging C-5s and C-141s. The tanker fleet—the air-to-air refuellers without which the combat craft cannot function—are also aging badly. Fortunately, the tanker fleet can be revived by converting Boeing 767 passenger aircraft to that use. Congress has approved a lease arrangement.[32]

Still, the Wasted Nineties witnessed some remarkable military statesmanship. After Desert Storm, Air Force Chief of Staff Merrill A. ("Tony") McPeak undertook a ruthless but necessary and effective consolidation of combat units and downsizing of the support establishment. Then in 1998, another chief of staff, General Michael Ryan decided to reconfigure the service. He implemented a concept known as the "Expeditionary Air Force," in which various units would be grouped into ten "Aerospace Expeditionary Forces" (AEFs), capable of rapid deployment to primitive—by Air Force standards—overseas facilities.

The AEF concept has proven very effective, managerially. Instead of grabbing units *ad hoc* as emergencies come up, or sending the same people to Saudi Arabia or over the Balkans again and again, units know when they'll be on-call and for how long. At the moment,

---

32. Frank Wolfe, "SAC Includes Lease Provision for 100 Tankers," *Defense Daily*, 5 December 2001, Early Bird.

the AEF concept is receiving its first wartime test, a test limited so far by the small number of bases available.[33]

Doctrinally and culturally, the AEF concept represents a major break with the past. AEFs are more than expeditionary aircraft packages, in many ways similar to an aircraft carrier's air wing or Marine air group. AEFs are also rapidly deployable packages intended to work with long-range bombers operating from distant fixed bases, capable of both independent operations and support of land campaigns. Naturally, not everybody in the Air Force seems happy. Many see AEFs as a resurgence of the "fighter mafia." The Navy and Marines also fly short-range aircraft, but only the Air Force possesses long-range bombers. The Air Force, these critics feel, should concentrate on what it alone can do.

You might think that the other services would view the AEFs as a sign that the Air Force, like the Navy, has done some reality testing and drawn the appropriate conclusions. They do. But a certain depth of resentment over real and perceived Air Force claims of supremacy lingers, as well as a considerable wariness, now that "Access" bids to become the fracas *du jour* and Air Force bombers are doing most of the airborne damage in Afghanistan.

There's another reason, already mentioned, why the other services—the Navy, especially—continue to regard the Air Force as on probationary good behavior. Air power zealotry has a certain Arnold Schwarzenegger quality: It'll be back. It's not often remembered that, on the eve of Desert Storm, Defense Secretary Dick Cheney fired Air Force Chief of Staff Michael Dugan for predicting (correctly, as it turned out) that air power would prove decisive in the war. General Dugan's successor, Merrill McPeak, kept quiet until after the war. Then the Air Force renewed and expanded its claims to independence and primacy. In a series of doctrinal statements, the Air Force went so far as to proclaim itself truly global by virtue of what it called "virtual presence."

Now, "presence," an ill-defined term that has something to do with letting folks know you're around, had rarely been an Air Force core competency. The planes flew over and it was all very impressive, and then you were left looking up into empty skies. If you

---

33. In fact, the demands of the Afghan campaign are already disrupting normal rotations. See "Jumper: The Mission Has Changed," *Air Force Times*, 10 December 2001, Early Bird.

AGAINST ALL TERRORS

wanted to intimidate the locals somewhere or influence a regional crisis, so the conventional wisdom ran, you needed a carrier group or other ships on-station, or boots on the ground. But now, USAF bombers operating from only three bases (in the United States, Guam, and Diego Garcia) could hit any spot on earth within eighteen hours of alert. Desert Storm proved it. Kosovo proved it. The Afghan campaign, with B-1s and B-52s operating off the Indian Ocean island of Diego Garcia, proves it. Still, presence, like beauty, is always in the eye of the beholder. (Navy advocates suggested that if airplanes could perform "presence" missions, subs could do so even more effectively, since nobody could ever be sure they weren't around.)

General McPeak's direct (many called it confrontational, arrogant, and worse) style of promoting the Air Force didn't help. By his final weeks, senior officers of other services were criticizing him loudly and publicly, writing group protest letters, and refusing to attend his farewell parties. His successor, General Ron Fogleman, provided a calming influence. Unfortunately, General Fogleman resigned midway through his tour in silent protest over the Clinton administration's handling of the Kelly Flinn adultery case and the Khobar Towers terrorist bombing.

Then came Halt.

And thus a perennial Air Force problem: the kind of distrust and *ressentiment* among the services that runs something like, "Yeah, you're behaving yourself now, but how long will it last this time?"

The obvious answer: It'll never go away entirely, this air power quest for ever greater utility. Nor should it. The title of the latest Air Force vision statement—*Global Vigilance, Reach and Power*—indicates that, as is human, dreams die hard.[34] Especially when they seem within reach.

And yet, the Air Force as presently constituted and acculturated has only a few more decades to live. During its first ten years as an independent service (1947 to 1957), the Air Force had to self-organize, fight the Korean War, manage the transition from piston aircraft to jets, devise a nuclear Strategic Air Command, develop long-range ballistic missiles, and start the trek into space. Over the next ten to

---

34. See also Maj. Gen. David A. Deptula, "US Air Force Transformation Will Expand the Nation's Strategic Options," *Armed Forces Journal International*, Oct. 2001, Early Bird.

twenty years, the Air Force will have to manage an even more difficult set of transformations.

The age of piloted combat aircraft is drawing to a close. In fifty years, maybe twenty-five, person-in-the-cockpit fighters and bombers will be as obsolete as the cavalry charge (although U.S. commandos working with the Northern Alliance participated in a few). The F-22 and the Joint Strike Fighter will probably be the last fighters built. It's not too much to imagine that some young cadet currently at the Air Force Academy will, as chief of staff, fly that last mission to some museum somewhere.

Bombers present a more complex problem. The current model B-2 may be the final bomber, although two options present themselves. The Air Force may consider reopening the production line for the B-2C or "B-2 Lite," a somewhat cheaper aircraft designed for conventional missions only. Northrop Grumman built the first 21 B-2s for about $44 billion. They claim they can put out 40 more for about $30 billion.[35] Others within the service argue for a final bomber that will have range and stealth, but carry less ordnance.[36] Curiously, the Air Force currently intends to shrink its current bomber fleet by retiring some of the B-1s, ostensibly to free up maintenance money for the rest.[37] This would do to the bomber fleet what has already happened to the navy's attack submarine fleet: reduce it far below minimum requirements.

Unfortunately, planes are expensive. When a single fighter can cost $200 million, when a single bomber can approach a billion, there is simply no way enough of them can be produced. As the saying goes, if it's too expensive to lose, it's too expensive to use . . . save under conditions approaching zero risk. So far, we've been lucky in the Balkans and over Iraq and Afghanistan. At the moment, the American aerospace system of systems—stealth, electronic warfare, etc.—is dominant. But it is possible to envision a world in which defense becomes ascendant. Stealth can be countered. Electronic warfare operations, such as suppression of enemy air defenses, are never

---

35. James Dao and Eric Schmitt, "New Pentagon Debate over Stealth Plane," *New York Times*, 11 December 2001, Early Bird.

36. Vago Muradian, "Roche: Air Force Needs New Stealthy, Fast, Long-Range Bomber, Not More B-2s," *Defense Daily*, 17 Oct. 2001, Early Bird.

37. Bruce Rolfsen, "Bombers Shine in Air War but Remain Budget Targets," *Air Force Times*, 26 November 2001, Early Bird. See also Thomas G. McInerney, "A Stealthy Transformation," *Washington Times*, 18 November 2001, Early Bird.

AGAINST ALL TERRORS

perfect and those assets—known in the trade as "High Demand/Low Density"—are over-stretched and wearing out. Also, the impending advent of effective directed energy weapons, from lasers to exotic particle beams, can create a battlefield environment in which nothing big can fly. Technological advances, which cannot be confined to the United States, may jeopardize or negate the air supremacy which we've taken for granted since World War II. It is not inconceivable that in a matter of years, expensive crewed aircraft could turn into so much high-tech junk.

Fortunately, there are now, as the Afghan campaign has shown, alternatives to piloted flight, most notably the Predator and Global Hawk UAVs (Uninhabited Aerial Vehicles). Yes, you need a person in the loop somewhere. But somewhere doesn't have to be the cockpit. UAVs are evolving rapidly as instruments of reconnaissance and surveillance. The Air Force is working on a pilotless bomber, aka Unmanned Combat Air Vehicle (UCAV). One form of testing has already begun. In October 2001, a Predator reconnaissance UAV was sent over Afghanistan armed with Hellfire anti-armor missiles. Results reportedly were mixed. In any event, Dr. Hans Mark, formerly the Pentagon's director of defense research, puts it simply: "[T]en years from now . . . we'll be building entirely different kinds of aircraft, namely robotic . . ."[38]

Another factor is nanotechnology and MEMS (Micro-Electro-Mechanical Systems). Current and next-generation UAVs are big: not as big as aircraft that have to support life, but big targets nonetheless. Micro-miniaturization tends toward UAVs the size of mosquitoes for intelligence gathering and targeting of remote weapons.

All this entails a wrenching cultural shift for the Air Force, a service dominated by aviators and wedded to the "white scarf and goggles" mystique. The Air Force likes to point out its functional diversity; less than a quarter of its present officer corps are pilots. Still, and despite all the fighter/bomber fussing, they rule. Who might supplant them?

The space folks, perhaps? Not likely, short-term. In truth, the Air Force has never accorded sufficient priority to, or been that comfortable with, space. Air Force doctrine speaks of aerospace as a "seamless environment," everything from the planet's surface on up, but the reality is different.

---

38. "Pentagon's Mark Sees Pilotless Future," *Defense Week*, 30 May 2000, Early Bird.

Space is a subject the Air Force approaches gingerly. *Global Engagement,* the service's most recent doctrinal statement, avows:

> The Air Force will sustain its stewardship of space and will fully integrate Air Force space capabilities in joint efforts to support the needs of the nation.

> The Air Force recognizes that any further use of space will be driven by national policy, international events, threats moving through and from space, and threats to U.S. space assets. However, the nation will expect the Air Force to be prepared to defend U.S. interests in space when necessary.[39]

Still, many analysts, and not a few folks on Capitol Hill, wonder whether the Air Force can make the institutional and cultural changes necessary to handle the coming revolution in space. At the moment, nearly all the Air Force's space (unclassified) projects can be described either as troubled or very troubled.[40] The Air Force counters that there's nothing wrong with its stewardship that money can't change; that it's committed to turning out junior officers capable of working in both realms; and that no institutional alterations are needed.[41]

Donald Rumsfeld disagrees. In May 2001, he assigned the Air Force primary responsibility for space and, very much to the point, directed that more space officers be promoted. The Air Force did not regard either directive with unrestrained ardor.

All in all, a strange situation for the world's premier air force. The Army, whatever its evolution, will still be the Army; the Navy will remain at sea. Only the Air Force, at the very moment of its triumph, has to face its own impending obsolescence and ponder a transition far more wrenching than those of the other services. The great challenge will be to manage the transition, keeping the piloted and crewed force strong for the next couple decades while accelerating the shift. And there's no reason why it can't be done, provided the Air Force remains true to its heritage of rapid innovation.

---

39. U.S. Air Force, *Global Engagement,* at www.af.mil
40. "Arnold: Most Big Space Programs Facing Cost, Schedule Difficulty," *Aerospace Daily*, 30 November 2001, Early Bird.
41. Sandra I. Erwin, "Air Force Articulates Strategy for Managing Space Program," *National Defense*, July 2000, Early Bird.

AGAINST ALL TERRORS

Marines

General Victor Krulak, a three-war Marine who almost became commandant in the 1960s, liked to say that the United States does not have a Marine Corps because the American people need one. In truth, the Army could take the Marines' job. We have a Marine Corps, "Brute" Krulak felt, because the American people want one. And they want one because they sense that it's good for the country in more ways than military.

And so it seemed when the Marines went into Afghanistan as the first major ground commitment. The Air Force bombers, the carrier strikes, the Army Rangers and Green Berets had been magnificent. But it was "The Marines have landed" that brought a sense of "and the situation is well in hand." General Krulak got it right.

So did his son. Chuck Krulak became commandant in 1995, at the height of the Clinton administration's assault upon the military. A decorated Vietnam and Desert Storm veteran, he held the line. While the other services lowered their recruiting standards and missed their quotas, the Marines raised their standards and exceeded their quotas. While the other services softened their co-ed boot camps, Marine boot camp stayed gender-segregated and got tougher for both. While the other services squabbled and fumed, Chuck Krulak enunciated a new kind of war. He called it the "Three Block War" and said over and over, "Just because it doesn't look like a war to me, that doesn't mean it's not a war."

This type of innovation is no new thing for the Marines. The disastrous British/Australian Gallipoli landings of the First World War generated a stiff conventional wisdom. Large-scale landings on defended beaches were suicidal and, even if the force did get ashore, it could not be sustained. But in the 1920s, then Commandant John Lejeune set the Marines to work developing the amphibious doctrine and techniques (including close air support of ground operations) that led to the great Marine and Army landings of World War II. In the 1980s, another commandant, General Al Gray, pioneered the "maneuver warfare" approach that changed the Corps' (and to some extent the Army's) concept of war, away from traditional and unimaginative attrition operation—the "body count" and "just take the turf" mentalities—and toward rapid destruction of the enemy's will and ability to mount organized resistance.

In like measure, General Krulak put the Corps to work against another stern dictum—conventional forces should never try to fight in cities. It's always bloody and rarely worth the cost. The Marines' two major post-World War II experiences in urban combat, Seoul in Korea and Hue City in Vietnam, left generations of officers swearing: Never Again. The Army's 1991 debacle in Mogadishu, Somalia, subject of the book and movie "Black Hawk Down," only added to the reticence. So did analysis of the Russian experience in Chechnya, especially the battles for Grozny. These demonstrated how easily forces designed for field combat could get chewed up by locals armed with rifles, grenades, rocket launchers, walkie-talkies, and not much more.

General Krulak concluded that since such combat was probably inevitable, we'd better learn to do it right. In any event, the Army was also working on MOUT, as Military Operations in Urban Terrain are known by their IA (Inevitable Acronym). He sensed that urban megasprawls, especially Third World coastal urban megasprawls, would be major twenty-first century battlefields. The "Three Block War" envisioned Marines and soldiers doing humanitarian operations on one block, acting as peace keepers and/or enforcers on the second, and fighting on the third.

But how to fight in cities against opponents who knew the physical and cultural territory, and who might have access to high-tech communications and possibly WMD? Old doctrine had little to say. So the Marines set up a special warfighting laboratory and launched the "Urban Warrior" experiments, including a mock invasion of Oakland, California. Initial results were mixed. Among the lessons learned: Hierarchical and rigid chains of command don't work as well as networks. The Marines are also "lead service" for developing non-lethal weaponry. Very useful when the armed enemy mingles with the civilian population, or when the civilian population is the problem. Better to hose down a crowd with Sticky Foam than with machine guns.

Of all the nation's military challenges, MOUT may prove the most difficult, requiring fundamental changes in tactics and relying on weapons that have yet even to reach the drawing board. The effort will make the development of large-scale amphibious assault—arguably the most intricate of all military activities—seem almost simple by comparison

Which brings us to what used to be called amphibious assault.[42] Forcible entry from the sea remains the Marines' primary statutory mission; the nation's amphibious capability resides in the Corps. But the classic landing, the stuff of Iwo Jima, is long gone. And frankly, good riddance. During World War II, amphibious planning often consisted of little more than finding a usable beach, which usually turned out to be a defended beach. Casualties were horrendous.

By the 1960s, "vertical assault" (helicopter operations) made it possible to bypass the beaches and go directly inland. Unfortunately, as the perils to the Marines decreased, dangers to their shipping and their helicopters mounted. Mines, missiles, and possible use of nuclear weapons made it impossible, or at least inadvisable, for naval task forces to go in close and stay there. Ship-to-shore resupply, the same. Ships no longer could linger for leisurely unloading; massive beach supply dumps were vulnerable. So the Marines and Navy evolved a new doctrine, "Operational Maneuver from the Sea," which emphasizes rapid movement from over-the-horizon and full exploitation of RMA intelligence and targeting assets. The latest iteration, *Expeditionary Maneuver Warfare*, continues the process:

> Twentieth century amphibious operations moved through distinct phases, pauses, and reorganizations. Twenty-first century expeditionary forces will be capable of moving directly from far offshore to objectives deep inland, uninterrupted by topography or hydrography, achieving greater surprise and complicating the adversary's defensive problem. . . .[43]

But this ability to strike deep and fast, in traditional parlance to hit 'em where they ain't, depends in large part on the much-maligned and most definitely troubled Osprey, a two-prop transport capable of vertical take-off and landing. With its longer range, greater payload, and flexibility, it will provide options unavailable with helicopters. Would that we'd had a few dozen in Afghanistan for Al Qaeda-chasing purposes.

Why bother maintaining this expensive amphibious capability? Perhaps because, to repeat, half the world's population and many potential battlefields reside within a hundred miles of some shore. Afghanistan may be landlocked. The next theater may not be. And in

---

42. See the Corps' doctrinal statement, *Operational Maneuver from the Sea: A Concept for the Projection of Naval Power Ashore*, at www.usmc.mil.

43. Taken from, William S. Cohen, Secretary of Defense, *Report to the Congress and the President 2001* (Washington, DC: GPO, 2001), p. 182.

the aftermath of 9/11, the Corps' present commandant, James Jones, established an anti-terrorism brigade of several thousand men and women, drawn from the Corps' existing counter-terrorism and security forces. At the time of establishment, the designated infantry component was 1/8, First Battalion, Eighth Marines—the outfit that went down when that suicide bomber hit their Beirut barracks back in 1983. Despite twenty years of talking about bringing that set of terrorists to justice, nothing has been accomplished. But memories die hard.[44] And in that part of the world, payback comes in many forms.

Space Force, Peace Force, Warriors, Guard

Each of the services faces a fundamental challenge: to transform itself so that its "core competencies" become effective in the twenty-first century as part of joint forces that achieve what the Pentagon calls "Full Spectrum Dominance." There are now many ways to do things. *Systems proliferate but effects converge.* There are now many new ways to create these capabilities across that spectrum—*versatility as a product of specialization plus mobility*. But these principles applied within the standard service/joint force matrix aren't quite enough.

Some analysts have suggested that maybe it's time for genuine unification, the creation of a single "American Defense Force" along the Israeli or Canadian models. All in all, probably not a good idea. Such arrangements only work when one form of combat power must dominate or when you don't have to fight at all. Merely pouring people into the same uniform does not eliminate internal conflict; in some ways, it intensifies it. Further, too much would be lost, especially those intangible but vital factors of tradition and *esprit*. What's needed is not unification, but a means of protecting and reifying new opportunities and capabilities. We call it here: "Space Force, Peace Force, Warriors, Guard."

---

44. Those conversant in military history may have noticed that the Marine force that went into southern Afghanistan in December 2001 was designated "Task Force 58"—the name of a much larger Navy/Marine force that did many of the great Pacific landings of World War II.

AGAINST ALL TERRORS

Space Force

Today, the United States is irrevocably dependent upon space for a variety of civilian and military uses. These uses are now irrevocably intertwined. Unfortunately, the Air Force has not been—and has not been permitted to be—an effective steward of space power.

Several reasons may be adduced. No post-World War II administration, including the present, has given the subject adequate attention. Most official pronouncements emphasized the peaceful exploration and utilization of space.[45] Several treaties and conventions purport to limit the "militarization" of space by banning the placement and testing of weapons of mass destruction in space. Whether these pacts would apply to less destructive weapons such as lasers is arguable. No administration since the sixties has sought adequate funding; money has come mostly out of Air Force and intelligence community accounts. Relations and co-operative ventures with NASA have been an on again/off again affair for decades, even as the civilian sector took the technological lead from the government. Finally, the Air Force argues that as long as what's up there just goes in circles and has no weapons capability, there's no need for a separate service.

Points well taken. But there is a need to start building now for the day when a separate service will be needed. Within a decade, there should be established a Space Corps within the Air Force, with its own budget "line item" and career paths. This should develop into a separate and independent Space Service within the Department of the Air Force, much as the Marines currently reside within the Navy Department. Three technological developments will determine the pace of that process. How fast will space-based assets acquire the capability to fight enemy space-based assets, offensively or defensively? How fast will the United States acquire an inexpensive "launch on demand" capability for both manned and unmanned vehicles? How long will it take to deploy a serious space-based ballistic missile defense system. This should belong to the Space Force, not the Army—a service with too much to do on earth.

---

45. For a good *précis* of this half century of neglect, see Steven Lambakis, *On the Edge of the Earth: The Future of American Space Power* (Lexington: University Press of Kentucky, 2001).

The subject of ballistic missile defense is complex and lies outside the scope of this book. But several points should be made. Surveys taken over the past thirty years indicate with astonishing consistency that the majority of the American people favor ballistic missile defense. But today, the United States does not have anything remotely resembling a successful system for the simple reason that success has never seriously been sought and might have been unwelcome, had it been achieved. Ronald Reagan never intended to build anything. His Strategic Defense Initiative was meant to bring the USSR to the bargaining table by forcing it to confront the prospect of wasting scarce resources to counter American initiatives. The tactic was called "competitive strategies." It worked. The senior Bush administration turned missile defense into, well, a typical government project, a set of sinecures scattered throughout the defense industry, the national labs, and an occasional university. The Clinton administration did the minimum to keep it alive whilst also setting it up to fail.

Today, however, a modest defense, capable of stopping a few missiles launched by a nation or organization other than China or Russia, is necessary. Yes, there are many other ways to attack the United States and yes, missiles do come "stamped with a return address." But missiles are still the most reliable means of wreaking mass death and destruction. And they pose a particular danger at the beginning and the end of crises and conflicts. At the beginning, they can intimidate; at the end, when an enemy may have nothing left to lose, they can avenge.[46]

9/11 has cost us trillions, directly and by its larger economic effects. Two buildings and a chunk of a third. How much more costly would be the destruction of an entire city, or five, or ten? Missile defense—effective defense against small strikes—must be developed now, and given in time to a Space Force that will both meet the needs of the other services and relieve them of burdens related to space.

Peace Force

"Great Powers Don't Do Windows."

---

46. See James M. Lindsay and Michael E. O'Hanlon, *Defending America: The Case for Limited National Missile Defense* (Washington, DC: Brookings Institution Press, 2001).

Sometime during Bill Clinton's tenure, this cutesy assertion became an unofficial slogan for a certain kind of officer, analyst, and pundit. The gravamen was that MOOTW—Military Operations Other Than War—were, save *in extremis* and only *in extremis,* unworthy of the United States and its military. No one objected to short-term humanitarian and disaster relief. Few questioned small-scale peace-keeping operations such as the Sinai, where the United States provided a couple hundred soldiers to police a treaty that both Israel and Egypt had wanted and signed. The hiccups came when the United States started getting involved, either deliberately or through "mission creep," in peace-enforcement: imposing peace on enemies who either didn't want or weren't ready for it.

Critics also noted that, historically, peace-enforcement usually led to taking sides with or against one faction or another, sometimes with disastrous results. The 1983 bombing of the Marine barracks at the Beirut airport happened only after the United States actively sided with the government in the Lebanese civil war. To most Lebanese, the government was simply one more faction. When the Sixth Fleet fired in support of government forces at the Battle of Suk el-Gharb, all perceptions of American neutrality vanished and U.S. forces became legitimate targets. Nine years later, the Mogadishu debacle came about after the U.S. humanitarian operation in Somalia had segued into a vendetta against one of the local warlords, Mohammed Farah Aidid. In both cases, attacks on American forces were followed by rapid and ignominious withdrawal.

The critics had other reasons to carp. MOOTW are enormously expensive and exhausting. The money to fund them was coming, as they say within the Beltway, "out of hide"—and the drain was accelerating the Defense Death Spiral. Further, these operations, especially in the Balkans, were open-ended. When senior officials spoke of staying in Bosnia "for as long as it takes," the question inevitably arose: for as long as it takes to do what? Convert the Balkans into peace-loving suburbs of NATO Europe?

And finally, the growing resistance to MOOTW bespoke a genuine snobbery. It wasn't just that messing in other peoples' domestics was ugly and costly and perilous. It wasn't just that Great Powers, no matter how great, needed to husband their resources, or that minor but well publicized defeats could have major ramifications. It was that the military genuinely did not *want* to do it. The whole debate came to resemble a conversation in Albert Camus' short story of the French Algerian War, "L'Hote." A rural police chief orders a teacher to take a prisoner to jail in a nearly town. The teacher demurs that it's not his job. The police chief counters, "In war one does all kinds of jobs." The teacher retorts: "Then I'll wait for the declaration of war!"

On 9/11, the declaration of war was delivered. Within a few weeks, it was already apparent that simply killing people and smashing things would not and could not guarantee the kind of foreign stability that militates against the growth of terrorism. Nor could the United States provide it by long-term physical occupation of foreign soil, or by simply pumping cash into such foreign governments as may come to pass in Afghanistan or elsewhere. Just as the whole array of military power must be available, so must the whole array of uses to which power might be put.

MOOTW, then, are neither sin nor salvation. They're activities the United States can expect to undertake from time to time. Therefore, the United States should prepare to conduct them with specialized forces, trained in MOOTW and adept at working in and with different cultures. This has two obvious advantages. It means more effective performance. And it frees combat forces to concentrate on combat. During the 2000 presidential campaign, when George W. Bush talked about an Army division receiving a "C-4" (not combat-ready) rating, the Army rightly responded that the division wasn't ready because too many of its critical assets were engaged in Bosnia.

Toward that end, the Army should establish a special active/ Guard/reserve Army Peacekeeping Command, which would provide the nucleus for future MOOTW. This command might be integrated into either the current Special Operations Command or placed within a new Counter-Terrorism Command, should one be established.

Forces assigned to MOOTW would not be, to borrow another phrase from the Wasted Nineties, "touchy-feely." They would be well-armed for the mission and capable of limited combat operations, i.e., offensive actions beyond self-defense. In most cases, these forces would operate in close co-ordination with or under civilian American authorities.[47] They would also make use of an array of non-military assets, from humanitarian NGOs (Non-Governmental Organizations) to the Professional Military Companies (PMCs) that increasingly

---

47. While such forces have been and will be part of international operations, command authority should be guarded jealously and never surrendered to the United Nations.

handle functions such as military, paramilitary, and police training on a contract basis. These enterprises, usually staffed by former U.S. military personnel, offer considerable expertise and skills that otherwise would have to be provided by the uniformed forces. They can also be paid out of non-defense accounts.

This Peace Force should be established *now*. The reason is that it will be needed within a year, perhaps two, certainly within three. In order to conduct a comprehensive offensive against Islamic Jihadism, the United States must impose and enforce an Israeli-Palestinian interim peace accord. This will require American boots on the ground to police the new borders and demilitarized zones and deal with other incidents. This will be a high-stakes, high-risk mission requiring unprecedented levels of military competence, cultural sensitivity, and non-military acumen. While other nations may participate, this is one time that American forces must dominate.

Warriors

These are the active, reserve, and National Guard units charged with combat missions, plus their essential supporting units. As the cliché goes, when they're not training to fight, they ought to be fighting. These units, whether legacy or interim or transformation forces, must achieve unprecedented levels of readiness and proficiency. They must not be distracted or frittered away.

Guard

As used here, the term "Guard" refers to all military forces, excluding ballistic missile and air defense, charged with the primary mission of protecting the American homeland, and such forces as may be assigned temporarily in time of emergency. It includes the Coast Guard and National Guard, but is not limited to them. The term implies that the role of the full-time active forces should be minimized, and that whenever possible the part-time citizen-soldiery should handle the necessary tasks. For this to work, several new levels of National Guard may have to be created. However, there is absolutely no need to return to federal conscription, and less than zero need to institute any system of compulsory national service with military and non-military "options."[48] Consideration of universal national service lies outside the scope of this book. However, suffice it to say that it would create a monstrous new bureaucracy. It would generate endless legal hassles. It would prove hideously unfair; guarding borders and getting shot at overseas are in no way commensurable with changing hospital bed pans or working in day care centers. It would take jobs from those who need them. And it would be, all in all, a typical government project.

The last thing this country needs is large quantities of young, mostly unskilled, and mostly resentful forced labor. There are better ways to go. Nor is it obvious that a period of national service would improve the moral character of the young. Many former draftees, now middle-aged or older, talk lovingly and often at far too great a length of how the draft turned them around, straightened them out, or otherwise adjusted their attitudes. Less frequent are the negative encomia—young people who had their lives screwed up (or ended) by the draft.

Prior to 9/11, the military's role in homeland defense was growing but still largely *ad hoc*. The Defense Department was only one of several dozen federal agencies directly involved, under the nominal co-ordination of a counter-terrorism "czar" on the National Security Council staff. Most defense support, real and potential, fell under the heading of "consequence management" and "support of civilian authorities," notably FEMA, the Federal Emergency Management Agency. In 1996, Congress established the Nunn-Lugar-Domenici Domestic Preparedness Program, authorizing the Defense Department to conduct instructional "visits" to fire and police departments in major cities.

Some worry that this program and others adopted after 9/11 violate the *Posse Comitatus* Act, which forbids the military to engage in domestic law enforcement under any circumstances. Actually, this bit of 1878 legislation, enacted to bar the use of federal troops as law enforcement agents in the South, does no such thing. Sometimes it seems that the more fervently some critics invoke this law, the less they understand it. Since the entire act consists of less than a hundred words, it's worth quoting in full:

---

48. See Charles Moskos and Paul Glastris, "This Time, a Draft for the Home Front, Too," *Washington Post*, 4 Nov. 2001, p. B-1.

From and after the passage of this act it shall not be lawful to employ any part of the Army of the United States as a *posse comitatus*, or otherwise, for the purpose of executing the laws, *except in such cases and under such circumstances as such employment of force may be expressly authorized by the Constitution or by act of Congress*; and no money appropriated by this act shall be used to pay any of the expenses incurred in the employment of any troops in violation of this section. And any person willfully violating the provisions of this section shall be deemed guilty of a misdemeanor and on conviction thereof shall be punished by fine not exceeding ten thousand dollars or imprisonment not exceeding two years or by both such fine and imprisonment."(Italics added)[49]

In truth, this "total" ban, which never existed anyway, has been steadily eroding for decades. In 1981, Congress passed the "Military Cooperation with Law Enforcement Officials Act," authorizing military aid in drug cases: the first of a series of laws and executive directives. In 1994, the Department of Justice and the Defense Department signed a memorandum of understanding on transferring military technology to civilian police departments. Other laws and directives, many highly classified, govern the military's domestic responsibilities in the aftermath of nuclear or terrorist attack.

By the latter nineties, then, every service was involved in various aspects of counter-terrorism and consequence management, often working in that gray area where law enforcement and defense meet and blur. Joint task forces proliferated. In 2000, the Norfolk, Virginia-based Joint Forces Command was given primary responsibility for homeland defense support. After 9/11, the JFC was authorized operational control of U.S.-based forces when engaged in homeland defense activities. In the aftermath, the Army considered establishing an Army Homeland Defense Command and the Defense Department pondered creating a Homeland Defense Command, along with a new under secretary of defense and several assistant secretaries.[50]

---

49. 10 USC 375. Chap 263, Sec. 15, enacted 18 June 1878. See Diane Cecilia Weber, "Warrior Cops: The Ominous Growth of Paramilitarism in American Police Departments," *Briefing Paper #50*, Cato Institute, 26 Aug. 99, p. 4.

50. See Yochi J. Dreazen and Davis S. Cloud, "Pentagon and White House Consider New Command against U.S. Attacks," *Wall Street Journal*, 21 November 2001, Early Bird; and Bradley Graham, "Military Favors a Homeland Command," *Washington Post*, 21 November 2001, Early Bird.

These ideas have merit, and should be implemented forcefully. Logically, the Army should be the lead service. Logically also, the Army National Guard should handle as much of the work as possible. After all, the Guard is already on-site. Its members know the territory and the people. Links to other state and local organizations are strong. However, effective use of the Guard would require both a major restructuring and fundamental cultural change—neither of which appeals to the present Guard establishment.

Since before the First World War, the National Guard has provided the bulk of the Army's combat power; the Army Reserve contains some combat units, but mostly holds support functions. Generations of Guard leaders have adopted a zero-tolerance policy toward any movement of the Guard away from combat. The "general purpose" mindset and the combat orientation are strong. Domestic functions, however important and time-consuming, are deemed lesser missions. And the Guard is keenly aware that, historically, the active Army's attitude tends toward a mixture of bemusement, contempt, and covetousness.

But not everyone. After Vietnam, Army Chief of Staff Creighton Abrams instituted one of the great visionary policies of the era. General Abrams restructured the Army so that, *by design*, it could not fight a major war without serious reserve and Guard mobilization. The rationale behind the "Abrams Doctrine" was clear. The Army could not go to war unless the government possessed the political will—and popular support—to engage the citizen-soldiery. This doctrine, quickly applied to the other services, became the "Total Force Policy" that worked so well during the Gulf War.[51]

Unfortunately, the Clinton administration perverted and suborned this doctrine by using Guardsmen and reservists extensively in MOOTW, especially in Bosnia. In an unusually candid moment, Defense Secretary William Cohen confessed that: "When possible, we use reserve forces to lift the burden from our first-to-fight units."[52] A policy designed to make sure the regulars didn't fight

---

51. One Army National Guard brigade mobilized for Desert Storm was never sent because they failed their pre-deployment "final exams." There is some evidence that Army leadership set the brigade up to fail, fearing that too much Guard success would reflect poorly on the standing forces and their budgets. See Lewis M. Sorley, "Roundout Brigades and the Gulf War: A Commentary," *National Guard Magazine*, May 1998.

AGAINST ALL TERRORS

major wars without the part-timers had morphed into a policy of relieving the active forces of their more distasteful missions.

At first, the Guard was happy to oblige, sensing a fine chance to prove their mettle and increase their appropriations. By decade's end, however, overuse was forcing people out and hurting recruitment. As a rule, reserve personnel should only be used for one long (more than thirty days) non-wartime overseas deployment during a career. Two or more within a few years is simply too disruptive of careers and families. Further, National Guard members have an unlimited liability for state duty. Too many call-ups, especially for perceived non-essentials, forces people out.

But even as the Pentagon was overusing the Guard in some ways, it was trying to gut it in others. The National Guard is organized into eight divisions and over a dozen separate brigades. Throughout the nineties, and despite the obvious and abysmal personnel shortfalls of the Two War Strategy, the Army claimed it could "find no mission" for the eight divisions. (By the end of the Clinton administration, some missions had been "found.") The active-duty folks preferred to concentrate on 15 or so "enhanced readiness brigades" that could fit into active divisions with post-mobilization training. Further, as Army transformation got underway, it became apparent that unless the Guard was also transformed, there would be a fundamental failure of "inter-operability." In other words, the better the active Army gets, the more obsolete large chunks of the Guard may become, at least insofar as they must operate with the active forces. The problem is real, and it grows ever more clear that not even the most advanced training methods—virtual reality, distance learning, etc.—can bridge the gap.

The solution may be to go with the principle that *specialization plus mobility yields versatility*. The enhanced brigade concept should be kept; a dozen or so of these brigades should be made as compatible as possible with their active counterparts. Other units should be redirected toward domestic missions. Perhaps some might be designated "domestic use only." The Army and the National Guard are considering a variety of short-term enlistment options (one or two years), which would provide people with adequate training for homeland

---

52. William S. Cohen, *Report to the Congress and the President 2000* (Washington, DC: GPO, 2000), p. viii.

duties, but not for foreign combat. These should be implemented on an experimental basis as soon as possible.

Simultaneously, the Guard and service reserves must capitalize on their great reservoir of civilian skills. The most obvious case: computers. The military can't pay enough to attract people with serious computer skills. But the citizen-soldiery has plenty. In recent years, large chunks of the military cyberwar (aka "information operations") mission have been given to reservists. So have a number of space-related functions. Other chronically and critically short specialties, from medicine to foreign languages, can be provided by reservists. But new programs, especially new commissioning programs, are needed to attract and retain them.

After 9/11, lots of young people visited their local recruiters. No great spike in enlistment ensued.[53] Perhaps just as well. Our most pressing need today may not be entry-level labor, but older men and women with special expertise. These people are long past their boot-camp years. But they could do great work as part-time specialists in special units.

A Final Word

Twenty-first century threats, as well as twenty-first century technologies, may empower eighteenth century virtues.

We live in a high-tech world. The military's becoming more and more high-tech. But what of the other part of the axiom? What virtues? Not patriotism *per se*: Anyone can feel that emotion. Not sacrifice, certainly not in the World War II manner. What virtue, then?

The virtue of willingness to provide for the common defense, to exercise both our responsibility and our right to do so. And this virtue begins with a special understanding—that defense is a continuum, not just something that is done by a certain group of people at certain times and in certain places and ways. The Founders understood this clearly. That's why they kept the notion of the "universal militia," of the populace in arms, even though militia units had performed not always well during the Revolution. That's why they assigned the "organized militia" both domestic law enforcement and military duties, and that's why the Second Amendment specifies that the right

---

53. Ironically, the services were already meeting their quotas, due to the shaky economy.

of the People ("People" being a legal term of art meaning "everybody") shall not be infringed. Most of the planet understands this continuum today, especially in places where the tidy distinctions we indulged prior to 9/11 have never availed.

The common defense begins with individual self-defense and defense of others. It extends to law enforcement, and to such actions as communities and local governments may undertake, perhaps even to the creation of new kinds of civil defense and paramilitary organizations. Only in its final forms does the common defense entail federal forces operating at home and abroad.

The citizenry may participate in the common defense in all these ways. Today, facing such a variety of threats, the citizenry must. As already mentioned, some are clamoring for renewed federal conscription or national service. A very bad idea: Coercion is not the way to go. Voluntarism is, at least until it can be shown that voluntarism alone won't meet the nation's needs. In November 2001, Senators John McCain and Evan Bayh introduced legislation expanding present volunteer opportunities. The Bush administration proposed a 20,000 person increase in groups such as AmeriCorps and Senior Corps. Their approach is correct: create new opportunities. Many cities and states and private organizations have already begun the task of organizing volunteers to meet various emergency needs: requirements often as relevant during a hurricane as during a terrorist attack. The job of classifying, training, and slotting these sundry volunteers can be difficult and frustrating. But it's far preferable to conscription.[54]

America's Guard, then, should consist ultimately of a population in which nearly everyone does, or is prepared to do, something. By all means, tier the National Guard and reserves to make room for specialists. Use them to the fullest extent possible, in order to minimize the federal effort. Over time, let state and local agencies organize the populace for emergency preparedness and response: a task that will pay fine dividends during natural as well as man-made emergencies. Make volunteer units of various kinds available for anyone who cares to join. Every high school student in the country should be required to

---

54. See Craig Savoye, "Volunteers Rally to Defend Their Homeland," *Christian Science Monitor*, 10 December 2001, Early Bird. See also Pam Belluck and Timothy Egan, "Cities and States Say Confusion and Cost Hamper Security Drive," *New York Times*, 10 December 2001, Early Bird.

learn basic First Aid and CPR, as well as what to do in event of attack.

The Wars of the Ways, then, will require major changes in the federal military role, but these should be kept to the necessary minimum. America's real Guard should be nothing less than a populace prepared to function as such, and bringing to the task their full complement of knowledge, skill and virtue.

4

Against All Terrors

Words matter. They matter because meaning, not force, is the essence of civilization. Force only defends it, or destroys it. In war, so runs a Roman proverb, the laws are silent. In war, so claims a modern proverb, truth is the first casualty. In war, so runs the common wisdom, violence sweeps reason away.

Not so. Whatever else may be said of war, it is a human activity and a human encounter. Reason and meaning still matter, in some ways even more than in time of peace. Weaponry, technology, courage, dedication—these provide the victories. But reason tells us what they're ultimately about: reason given form in words.

Words of reason are no new thing for Americans. They're the way we've expressed our commitments in the world. Many times, we've said what we meant, meant what we said, and then gone out and done it. Our commitments have come in many forms. There was the Founders' mutual pledge of life, fortune, and sacred honor. There was Lincoln's Gettysburg rededication. There was the "Day of Infamy" commitment. The goals were clear, the resolve unarguable.

Then there are what John Kennedy so rightly called the "long twilight struggle" commitments. The goals are more nebulous, the resolve more subject to vicissitude. Ten years ago, the United States concluded a half-century twilight struggle against communism. Whether we won in some grand and satisfying fashion, or merely outlasted the foe, is immaterial here. What matters is that, despite any number of failures and stupidities and missed opportunities and domestic rancor, we won. And whether the world cares to admit it or not, the world is a better place because of it.

Today, the American people overwhelmingly support the campaign to destroy Al Queda. It's a "Day of Infamy" thing. But soon enough, the battle against Islamic terrorism will segue into twilight struggle. Long twilight struggle, against the as-yet innumerable other terrors that this century may send our way. And if it be true that the planet has indeed entered the Age of the Wars of the Ways, it's an age we've still to begin to ponder, and whose final cost we cannot even start to comprehend. "Day of Infamy" resolve has been forced upon us. The resolve necessary for long twilight struggles must be crafted and nurtured and maintained.

We've done it before. There's no reason why we can't do it again. Many doubt that a nation so conflicted culturally, so far gone in Political Correctness and (to some, anyway) moral decadence, can gird up for the strife and stay girded. Nonsense. The necessary qualities of civic virtue belong to no particular group or ideology or persuasion. People of all understandings may choose to serve, according to their abilities and opportunities, as guardians of the twenty-first century. But it's necessary to be clear about two things: what level of commitment may be necessary, and what the vital virtues are.

History contributes to clarity. We twenty-first century Americans have an unusual relationship to the past. Unlike most other peoples, we're free to ponder it without being bound by it. History does not tell us what to do, or whom we must succor or slay. We're free to assemble our own pastiche of lessons and maxims, free to create a "usable past" out of whatever combinations work. We end, therefore, with two items from the "usable past." One recalls the last time the United States forged a twilight struggle consensus. The other recalls a certain little-remarked aspect of the Founding Fathers' approach to civic virtue. It may seem an odd pairing. But taken together, they offer a guidance worth considering.

The Cold War Commitment

America in 1946 had issues. The Second World War had ended the year before, and if the postwar world was not providing disasters in the ways expected—a new depression, combat veterans running amok in the streets, women refusing to turn their jobs back to the men—it was still a troublesome time. A nation that had lived through fifteen years of stress and peril and a couple million wartime "We regret to inform you" (son, father, husband, brother/ dead, wounded, missing) telegrams finally received the opportunity to make money and babies at will. They did both with commendable gusto.

Yet even then, there were indicators that the future might turn difficult in unanticipated ways. Feminist Betty Friedan's *Feminine Mystique* and the "Problem without a Name" and the great debates over the soul-numbing tackiness of mass culture lay a decade ahead. So did the whole "Whatever Happened to the American Male?" lamentation of the fifties, the "Organization Man" jeremiads, the conformity frets.[1] So did the civil rights movement's determination to call in an IOU signed by Abraham Lincoln. Soon enough, all this and much

---

1. Yes, the issue of the "demasculinization" of the American male first arose in the 1950s. Actually, it revived a theme from the Progressive Era.

AGAINST ALL TERRORS

more would converge across the generations to provide the critical mass that ignited a Thirty Years Culture War. Such a conflict was, no doubt, unimaginable back then. Still, even as the business of breeding and the breeding of business accelerated, there were forebodings.

The first great surge of veterans into politics came in 1946. Many, including a former Navy officer named John Kennedy who was running for Congress, campaigned on the need for postwar unity—a need driven as much by recent memories and emotions as by future perils. The terms "post-traumatic stress disorder" and "chronic stress disorder" wouldn't make it into the *Diagnostic and Statistical Manual*, the official encyclopedia of dysfunction put out by the American Psychiatric Association, for three more decades. But in 1946, these and myriad other problems with as yet no names were already taking their toll. America's veterans, candidate Kennedy asserted, felt "alone." Others claimed that the nation itself, so recently so resolute, was adrift.

In terms of world affairs, this was so. When the war ended, the United States had twelve million men and women under arms. Demobilization had proceeded rapidly and, from a military point of view, idiotically. Instead of disbanding by units, veterans were released as individuals, based on a complex point system that assigned values to length of service, overseas time, combat time, family status, and other factors. Politicians endured extreme pressures to speed up the process—"No Boats, No Votes," as the slogan ran. By the 1946 election, the United States possessed less usable military power than at any time since the mid-1930s, and would not begin to rectify this neglect until the Korean War. America had a monopoly on the atomic bomb (which would end in 1949, several years ahead of the CIA's expectation), but after Hiroshima and Nagasaki we'd stopped building them and dismantled the Manhattan Project. We were, or at least we seemed to be, both irresolute and weak.

The Russians didn't seem weak. Nor did they seem lacking in resolve. At a 1946 Congressional hearing, General Omar Bradley was asked what the USSR would need to march from central Europe to the English Channel. His answer: "Boots." In truth, the Soviet Union was victorious but exhausted. The extent of Soviet weakness would not be fully known for many years. Twenty million dead in the war; at least that many dead from Stalin's purges; European Russia laid waste; a new empire to garrison, resistance movements to put down;

no more American aid. In reality, the Soviet boots weren't there. But then, there weren't a whole lot of Americans still in their boots, either. All anybody knew for sure was that the wartime Soviet ally, so recently the subject of so many flattering articles and newsreels, had devolved into a postwar peril: truculent, oppressive, unyielding.

It was scary, this novel tandem of chronic foreign stress and burgeoning domestic prosperity. It was also bewildering. Even the government thought so. So in 1946, the State Department asked George Kennan, a young American diplomat then serving as *chargé d'affaires* at the U.S. embassy in Moscow, to explain why the Soviets were behaving so brutally and imperiously. Mr. Kennan replied in a classified cable that went down in diplomatic history as "The Long Telegram." A version appeared in the July 1947 issue of *Foreign Affairs* under the pseudonym "X," which went down in diplomatic history as the "X Article," even though the author's identity was soon revealed. Kennan's essay, "The Sources of Soviet Conduct," proved once again that words matter; that ideas have consequences; and that to succeed an idea must be more than true. It must also fit the civilization that receives it.

His analysis was elegant. The Soviets were suffering from a set of interlocking delusions about the world that, unfortunately, they couldn't live without. Because of the way they saw things, wrote Kennan, ". . . there can be no appeal to common mental approaches."[2] Self-serving illusions, not rational perception, guided their conduct.

First, the Russians were Russians, heirs to a long history of foreign invasion and oppression, and to a harsh tradition of xenophobia. They were congenitally paranoid. Regardless of whatever we might do to reassure them of our benign intent, their suspicions would survive. Second, we could not convince them of our benign intent because they were also Marxists who viewed the capitalist world as inevitably "hostile and incorrigible," fit only for expropriation and destruction.[3] Third, they were messianics. Pre-communist Russia had long thought of itself as the "Third Rome," sacred repository of the only true Christianity. Three Romes, the saying went: the original, the Byzantine, the Russian. Three and there will be no fourth. As Marxists, they considered themselves the vanguard of an inevitable world

2. George F. Kennan, "The Sources of Soviet Conduct," reprinted in George F. Kennan, *American Diplomacy*, Expanded Edition (Chicago: University of Chicago Press, 1979), p. 118.
3. Ibid, p. 112.

revolution, so inevitable that they were in no great Hitlerian frenzy to bring it about. Finally, Stalin and his ilk were ugly, brutal tyrants, requiring a foreign enemy to explain away their own failures and justify their own authority and repressions.

However, Kennan argued, the fact that they were deluded didn't mean they were crazy. They were, all things considered, rather cautious and very capable of understanding power relationships. When confronted, they'd back off. Then, in a passage that both predicted and provided the *leitmotif* of the next four decades, he suggested that:

> . . . Soviet pressure against the free institutions of the Western world is something that can be *contained* by the adroit and vigilant application of counter-force at a series of constantly shifting geographical and political points, corresponding to the shifts and maneuvers of Soviet policy, but which cannot be charmed or talked out of existence.[4] (Italics added.)

And thus arose the doctrine of containment, the essence of American Cold War strategy. Other documents and other actions made containment official policy and strategy. But Kennan had provided the words that brought it all together. He'd explained what the Soviets were about and why, and although his explanation missed a lot of nuance, it was essentially correct. He'd recommended a prudent response that required neither total mobilization nor promiscuous globalization.[5] And just as important, he advocated a response that would resonate with the American people as they were, materially and culturally, in the latter 1940s:

"Surely," he concluded, "there was never a fairer test of national quality than this. In the light of these circumstances, the thoughtful observer of Russian-American relations will find no cause for complaint in the Kremlin's challenge to American society. *He will rather experience a certain gratitude to a Providence which, by providing the American people with this implacable challenge, has made their entire security as a nation dependent on their pulling themselves together and accepting the responsibilities of moral and political leadership that history plainly intended them to bear."*[6] (Italics added)

---

4. Ibid, p. 120.
5. In Kennan's original formulation, containment was neither global nor primarily military; he often bemoaned the forces that led to the "defeat anywhere is a defeat everywhere" mindset and the Vietnam trauma.
6. Ibid, p. 128.

Thank God for the Russians? Not exactly. Nor did Kennan indulge himself in "Pay any price, bear any burden" exhortations. That too would come later. Rather, Kennan's words provided America with a carefully delineated and limited mission. Containment was real-world necessity. Containment provided a clear and gratifying national purpose. But it demanded no crusade and it mandated no Third World War. It was, in many ways, a strategy for avoiding war. Containment was perfect for a nation uneasy over its self-perceived lack of purpose, yet unwilling to put its boots on again.

How perfect? Good enough to endure when the nuclear arms race made the price of failure either World War III or a totalitarian New Dark Age. Good enough to guide the nation through the 1980s end game, a period whose hazards are only now starting to become apparent. And good enough that victory brought no jingoistic self-exaltation, only relief and a genuine well-wishing to a Russian people whom we'd never hated, whom we'd often admired, and whom we need today as partners in the Wars of the Ways.

By now, the parallels between what Kennan did and what must be done should be obvious. In many ways, the *Jehadi* (religious, ideological, racial, ethnic, and otherwise) of the twenty-first century are and will be like the Soviets: locked into a set of delusions that they neither can nor choose to shed. In many ways, their delusions will resonate with the desperate billions of this planet. But how strong are they, really? The evidence of 9/11 and since would seem to indicate they're both weaker and more dangerous than we might have thought. Some *Jehadi* may embrace the psychopathic or the suicidal, but it is far more likely that most will adapt an outlook best expressed by that old bit of doggerel: He who hits and runs away lives to fight another day.

Kennan's doctrine of containment might not seem entirely apt here. Hard-core terrorist *Jehadi* cannot be contained; they must be neutralized. But the key point here is not containment; it is self-containment. The United States cannot and should not run around the planet, shooting up everything that looks suspicious. Power must be used effectively and precisely, and in a manner that teaches lessons. But there will be times and reasons when power should not be employed, even against enemies. Long twilight struggles also require limitation and restraint.

But what of Kennan's final peroration? Did 9/11 offer us a chance to "pull ourselves together as a nation," cast aside our differences, and get about it? No, of course not. It's not that kind of struggle—not yet, anyway. "Disaster as redemption" we can do without. And the struggle does not require coercive sameness to win. In fact, rather the opposite. To the extent that our national preoccupation with diversity has made us more aware of the differences and grievances of others on this planet, that's all to the good. In the decades ahead, it will be vital to know where they're coming from and why, even when we disagree or choose not to honor their requests and demands . . . or respond to their insults. No, what is needed is not sameness, or patriotism, or invocations of sacrifice. What is needed is civic virtue, at least enough of us with enough virtue to prevail. Whence cometh such virtue? A look at the Founders reveals something both astonishing and characteristically American.

The Founding Fear

"We have, probably, had too good an opinion of human nature in forming our confederation."[7]

So wrote George Washington in 1785. What has this comment on the failings of the confederal government, that which ran the United States from the beginnings of the Revolution until the adoption of the federal Constitution, to do with the matters at hand?

Everything—if the connection be properly understood. The connection here is the matter of virtue, specifically civic virtue, and more specifically the human ability to participate meaningfully and effectively in the common world and, as part of that participation, to provide for the common defense.

Few items engaged the intellects and anxieties of the Founders more than the virtue of the citizenry. "A republic, if you can keep it," Benjamin Franklin is reputed to have said to a man who asked him what kind of government, republic or monarchy, the Constitutional Convention had brought forth. "If you can keep it"—both admonition and confession of very serious doubt. Indeed, much of the history of this nation can be read as a complex counterpoint of self-esteem and self-doubt (both to some degree dystrophic). We're the Elect, the Vis-

7. Quoted in Gordon S. Wood, *The Creation of the American Revolution: 1776–1787* (Chapel Hill: University of North Carolina Press, 1969), p. 472.

ible Saints of the City on a Hill, the greatest nation that ever was or ever will be. Or are we? Effusive self-praise and censorious self-flagellation have long co-existed in the American soul. Both attempt to answer the same endlessly vexatious question: Are we—can we be—good enough? From Puritan jeremiads to *New York Times* editorials; from Manifest Destiny to Indispensable Nation, the concern remains the same.

Are we good enough?

The question will never be answered definitively, at least not so long as there's a United States to ask it. The mere fact that it's posed so incessantly in so many different ways, and susceptible to so many contradictory answers, would indicate its fundamental opaqueness. But the American Revolution and the years leading to the Constitutional Convention established a pattern that remains relevant today.

The American Revolution was a curious affair. "The Americans," writes historian Gordon Wood, "were not an oppressed people; they had no crushing imperial shackles to throw off. In fact, the Americans knew that they were probably freer and less burdened with cumbersome feudal and hierarchical restraints than any part of mankind in the eighteenth century."[8]

Taxation without representation is tyranny, they claimed. But it wasn't. The vast majority of Britons, who paid far higher taxes, weren't represented in Parliament, either. Under the British doctrine of "virtual representation" which held that every member of Parliament represented and legislated for the whole, this colonial rally-cry seemed questionable at best. Royal plots to "reduce them under absolute despotism"? King George III was merely functioning as an enlightened eighteenth century monarch, intent upon rationalizing his administration and maybe getting back some of the money he'd spent driving the French out of much of North America.

Given this relative paucity of oppression, many historians have concluded that it was all economic. The colonies could simply make more money as independent states, and not a few colonists would be quite happy to let the war nullify their debts to British banks and merchants. While the explanation may have some value, it founders on one fact. Britain was the most powerful empire on earth. To oppose her was a very serious undertaking, a long shot at best. And the standard British punishment for treason was a multi-part affair, of which

---

8. Wood, *Creation*, p. 3.

AGAINST ALL TERRORS

the last and least unpleasant segment was either hanging or beheading after having been hung almost to death.

If it wasn't about oppression, and it wasn't about economics, what would drive men to risk their lives, their fortunes, and their sacred honor for eight perilous and straitened years? The answer may well be a strange anxiety that, unless they revolted, they would never be *good enough*. Writes Wood:

> What ultimately convinced Americans that they must revolt in 1776 was not that they were naturally and inevitably republican, for if that were truly the case evolution, not revolution, would have been the eventual solution. *Rather it was the pervasive fear that they were not predestined to be a virtuous and egalitarian people* that in the last analysis drove them to revolution in 1776. . . .
>
> When the Americans examined themselves in the years leading up to the Revolution, it became apparent that their society had been undergoing a drastic and frightening transformation. All the signs of the society's development by the middle of the eighteenth century, as described in the language of the day, became symptoms of regression. (Italics added)[9]

What signs? At home, a growing obsession with materialism or, in the language of the day, "luxury." For some, loss of religious ardor. For many, especially among the more privileged white males, an ever-increasing unwillingness to bear arms in the common defense, as witnessed by the decline of the colonial militia system. Rampant selfishness and concern for purely private affairs. And most of all, the failure to resist what their instincts told them was a British conspiracy to strip them of both their rights as Englishmen and their special colonial liberties a bit at a time. As historian Bernard Bailyn points out in his classic *Ideological Origins of the American Revolution*, from the "unenlightened" colonial perspective, the home country had already surrendered to tyranny. Unless the colonists took immediate action, they'd be next. As Bailyn puts it:

> Liberty was not, therefore, for the colonists, as it is for us, professedly the interest and concern of all, governors and governed alike, but only of the governed. The wielders of power did not speak of it, nor did they naturally serve it. . . . [T]he preservation of liberty rested on the ability of the people to maintain effective checks on the wielders of power. . . .

---

9. Ibid, pp. 107–108.

It was this, the overwhelming evidence, as they saw it, that they were faced with conspirators against liberty . . . that was signaled to the colonists after 1763, and it was this above all else that in the end propelled them into Revolution.[10]

As paradoxical as it might sound, the colonies rebelled out of fear that they might not be people of sufficient virtue to rebel . . . not good enough. The notion may not satisfy the American Psychiatric Association's diagnostic criteria, but it helps explain why they would run such enormous risks in response to such comparatively mild provocations. It also explains certain mostly forgotten actions of the First Continental Congress, which amounted to an attempt to by the government to legislate the renewal of civic virtue via restrictions upon what we now call life-style. As historian Ann Fairfax Withington writes:

> In 1774, the Congress took a stand: no more horse-racing, no more cockfighting, no more playing cards, no rolling dice, no more gaudy dressing, no more theatre. . . . For colonists in 1774, the way to virtue was through discipline. . . . Congress was concerned to render people fit members of society.[11]

The various colonial non-importation movements had a similar intent. American refusal to purchase British luxury goods had less to do with whacking the mother country's economy than with demonstrating stern republican self-discipline and resolve. On the eve of a vicious war with the most powerful empire on earth, the revolutionaries apparently needed reassurance that they were at least capable of giving up British hats and fancy funerals.

But why should they need such reassurance? Why were they so lacking in the absolute certainty so often attributed to revolutionaries? Why were they so afraid they weren't *good enough*?

The Founders read history, especially the classics. They read history very seriously. They knew how rare a commodity civic virtue was, and how difficult to sustain. But they also knew that, from time to time, the people could be roused to greatness. To quote Wood:

> Everyone was intensely aware of the special character of republicanism and the social and moral demands it put upon a people. . . .

---

10. Bernard Bailyn, *The Ideological Origins of the American Revolution* (Cambridge: Harvard University Press, 1967), pp. 59, 65, 95.

11. Ann Fairfax Withington, *Toward a More Perfect Union: Virtue and the Formation of American Republics* (Oxford: Oxford University Press, 1991), pp. 13, 77.

That the greatness, indeed the very existence, of a republic depended upon the people's virtue was a "maxim" established by "universal consent" and the "experience of all ages. . . ."[12]

The decision to rebel, then, was a desperate gamble that they could indeed be good enough. "Only this faith in the regenerative effects of republican government itself on the character of the people can explain the idealistic fervor of the Revolutionary leaders in 1776. . . . The Revolution with all its evocation of patriotism and the martial spirit would cleanse the American soul . . ."[13]

Disaster as redemption? No. Self-governance as redemption. Accepting responsibility as redemption. Standing up before the "opinions of mankind" and taking the consequences of war as redemption.

Were they good enough? Yes, they were, enough of them, to wage and win an eight year war. Were they redeemed? Not hardly. They emerged thoroughly cleansed of any illusions about the American ability to sustain mass civic virtue for long periods.

Nor did the years between 1783 and 1787 enhance their estimate. As Wood writes in *The Radicalism of the American Republic*: "The founding fathers were unsettled and fearful not because the American Revolution had failed, but because it had succeeded, and succeeded only too well. . . . White males had taken only too seriously the belief that they were free and equal with the right to pursue their happiness."[14] The nation returned to rampant pursuit of luxury and self-interest; state governments faltered; the "wrong men" were getting both rich and powerful. It seemed to Washington and others that the Revolution, itself an escape from corruption, had merely generated additional opportunities for its exercise.

Seen in this sense, the Constitution represented a confession of moral failure. It was not a failure that would have surprised the Founders, men with a somber sense of the limits of human virtue. But it was a failure nonetheless. As Withington writes, the United States became "a republic founded on the sovereignty of a people, not on their character—on balanced interests, not on virtue."[15] The Constitu-

---

12. Wood, *Creation*, pp. 91–92.
13. *Ibid*, pp. 120–121, 124.
14. Gordon S. Wood, *The Radicalism of the American Republic* (New York: Knopf, 1992), p. 368.
15. Withington, *Union*, p. 249.

tion is justly revered for the brilliance of its "checks and balances," creating "a machine that would go of itself" by the artful counterpoise of interests, and by the addition of a Bill of Rights designed primarily to limit the powers of the federal government, not endlessly enhance the liberties of the individual. But the Constitution nowhere mentions virtue, not even in the Preamble. Had the Founders given up entirely and placed their trust in the gizmos of government?

Not at all. Civic virtue mattered more than ever. But the Founders made a conscious decision not to use the federal government as a "school of virtue." The republic would not involve itself in the business of producing virtuous citizens. That would be done elsewhere—in families, churches, schools, communities, voluntary organizations, and in the exercise of three great collective rights and obligations: voting, jury duty, and militia service. In his Farewell Address, Washington avowed that: "Of all the disposition and habits which lead to political prosperity, religion and morality are indispensable supports." But the religion he invoked was a "civil religion" that impelled citizens toward a sense of obligation, not an enforceable theology. And when he mentioned morality, he was not urging abstinence education or tobacco awareness, but a sense of personal responsibility that possessed both private and public components.

In sum, the Founding Fathers, knowing full well from both history and their own lives how vital, how precious, and how rare sustained civic virtue was, nonetheless refused to let the federal government teach it or compel it. No Pledge of Allegiance, no "In God We Trust" on the money, no national anthem, no loyalty oaths. All that came later, in subsequent iterations of the *Are We Good Enough?* torment. No, the Founders took a gamble at least as audacious as the Revolution itself. But they knew that, in the end, that which was most essential was also the least likely to be compelled.

Or manipulated.

And thus began a centuries-long American wonderment, which may have no parallel in human history. Many nations, many peoples have felt and proclaimed their superiority, bewailed their inferiority, and done both simultaneously. But this often obsessive introspection—*Are We Good Enough?*—seems uniquely American. At times, clearly, enough of us were good enough; the Civil War and Greatest Generations come to mind. At times there have been leaders who demanded our best: Lincoln, both Roosevelts, JFK in his flawed and tragically aborted way. And there have been times and leaders when something rather the opposite has prevailed, when we've supported and succored leaders who asked too little; who've appealed too much to our own lesser natures; and who left us with an uneasy sense of, "What were we thinking of when we let that man govern us?" And there have been leaders who knew what to ask for, and when to stop. Eisenhower was such a man. Perhaps George W. is, too.

So what's the point? Simply this. It is not enough to possess the power to wage the Wars of the Ways. It is not enough to commit the nation to it. It is only enough to possess the power and the commitment, and to be worthy—to be *good enough* to serve as some of the guardians of the twenty-first century.

What does this mean? What should it mean? There are no one-size-fits-all prescriptions. Power comes in many forms. So does commitment. So does worthiness. I suggest that this new national quest for worthiness has already begun. It has not begun because a few Culture Warriors have decreed that patriotism and morality are once again "in fashion"—a term itself signifying only the transient and the trivial. It has begun via a growing unwillingness to condone many things this civilization has become, or any longer to excuse its failures.

Since 9/11, when you channel surf, do you come across programming that is, in some vague disturbing way, unworthy of us?

When you ponder some of this country's more lunatic material excesses, do you find that too unworthy?

When you listen to all the stale clichés and jeremiads that fill the media and the schools and the pulpits, do you find that too unworthy?

If you've grown ever more uneasy with this civilization of Nothing Matters and Anything Goes and Who Are You to Judge, then you're doing what the Founders hoped, in every generation, somehow, enough of us would do.

Realize that, in the end, *our wars and our ways are inextricably connected.*

A few weeks after 9/11, the Advertising Council released a commercial at least as moving as it was saccharine. It showed people of every race, religion, gender, ethnicity, accent, dress, one after another saying the same four words. I am an American.

Who am I to judge the condition of this civilization as it enters the Wars of the Ways? I am an American. Who are we to judge? We are Americans—for all our faults and failings, once again the guardians of human potential and hope, should we choose to accept this new twilight struggle, and should we choose to be worthy of it.

Power we may generate and use in all its forms. Worthiness also we are free to generate, in all its forms. And persistence, also, the persistence appropriate to a struggle in which there will be seasons of victory, days of disaster, and long periods of nothing (seemingly) at all. Taken together, power—the ability to act—and worthiness—the right to act—may generate courage, the special courage of those with a great work to accomplish. Plato once defined courage as endurance of the soul. Millennia later, Ernest Hemingway called it grace under pressure.

A civilization of power and worthiness and persistence is a civilization of courage. It is fit to wage the Wars of the Ways. And it will stand against all terrors.

Appendix A
Readings and Browsings

In the summer of 1999, as the Wasted Nineties trended down, the release of a Gallup Poll occasioned a few eyebrow exercises in the national security world. The survey revealed that 43 percent of the American people felt "they don't get enough data about the military to be informed citizens."[1] Despite all the apathy and cynicism of that decade, despite all the alleged "estrangement" between the military and civilian worlds, nearly half wanted to know more. Interestingly, only 28 percent said they wanted to know more about the military's sexual scandals, dilemmas, and malfeasances.

Also of note—89 percent of the reporters surveyed said that what the public really wanted was sex. Their fellow citizens were lying.

Since 9/11, there's been a lot less news about military sex scandals, and a lot more about what the military really is and does. Unfortunately, all the popular media coverage, no matter how accurate and earnest, adds up to less than the sum of its parts. Context is lacking.

Fortunately, there's also a lot of good stuff out there. You need not depend on what the popular media get around to reporting, and repeating and repeating and repeating. The purpose of this section is to provide a barely minimal reading list for context, then some suggestions on how to learn more and stay current, i.e., which web sites to hit.

No attempt is made to rate the major TV networks or the all-news stations. Although their coverage has improved significantly since the 1980s (and certainly since the 1960s), they'll never really get it right. The subject is simply too complex for the sound-bite approach and the constraints of a general audience. However, there are some first-rate individuals. Jamie McIntyre of CNN and John McWethy of ABC come to mind as personal favorites. And from time to time, all the major TV networks do good-to-excellent features. So do the more specialized cable channels: Discovery (no relation to Discovery Institute), TLC, and the History Channels, especially. This list is far from exhaustive.

Nor is any attempt made to rate the quality of print reporting, except to note that there are some excellent reporters out there.

---

1. John Donnelly, "Public Not Interested in Military, Especially Sex Lives," *Defense Week*, 7 September 1999, p. 16.

Michael Gordon of the *New York Times* and Tom Ricks of the *Washington Post* are both savvy veterans. So is John Fialka of the *Wall Street Journal*. In recent years, Bill Gertz of the *Washington Times* has become something of a "designated leak" for the CIA and other agencies. Among the more liberal set, William Broad, Molly Moore, and William Arkin, all of the *Washington Post*, are worth reading.

Ten (or Twelve) Basic Books

1. The indispensable primer is Martin van Crevald's *The Transformation of War* (Free Press). Van Crevald, an Israeli historian of international stature and the author of a dozen other noted works, can get a bit too erudite at times. Still, he tells it like it is, and as it will be.

2. Another book that tells is like it is comes from Edward Luttwak. Although *The Pentagon and the Art of War* (Simon & Schuster/ICS) appeared in 1984, it's still an apt diagnosis of the defense establishment's systemic flaws, shortcomings, and frustrations. Luttwak, a defense analyst at the Center for Strategic and International Studies in Washington, DC, has a number of other major military works to his credit.

3. James Fallows' *National Defense* (Random House), also appeared in the 1980s, but remains relevant as a primer on how defense reform does and doesn't happen. Fallows, a journalist with no military experience, was chosen by the leaders of the pre-Desert Storm defense reform movement to produce an accessible general-audience book. *National Defense* and *The Pentagon and the Art of War* are also useful reminders, not just of what's wrong, but of how far we've come.

4. The next book comes from Donald Kagan, a Yale military historian and renowned classicist, and his son Frederick. *While America Sleeps: Self-Delusion, Military Weakness, and the Threat to America Today* (St. Martin's) appeared in 2000, and falls into the category: more relevant now than ever.

5. This anthology addresses military transformations in historical context. Williamson Murray, editor, *The Dynamics of Military Revolutions: 1300—2050* (Cambridge University Press) might get a bit detailed for general readers, but is nonetheless worth the time.

6. *Lifting the Fog of War* (Farrar Straus & Giroux) by retired Navy Admiral Bill Owens is a genuine must-read: clear, direct, and written by a man who lived it. During his career, Owens, a submarine officer by training, also commanded the U.S. Sixth Fleet in the Mediterranean. As a Deputy Chief of Naval Operations in the early nineties, he was instrumental in beginning the Navy's transformation. Later, as Vice Chairman of the Joint Chiefs of Staff and Chairman of the Joint Requirements Oversight Council, he attempted to bring some sanity to the defense development and procurement processes. His recommendations are sound.

Three more books deal with specific issues not covered in this book.

7. Cyberwar: James Adams, *The Next World War—Computers Are the Weapons and the Front Line Is Everywhere* (Simon & Schuster).

8. Biowar: Judith Miller, Stephen Engelberg and William Broad, *Germs: Biological Weapons and America's Secret War* (Simon & Schuster).

9. Missile defense: James M. Lindsay and Michael E. O'Hanlon, *Defending America: The Case for Limited Missile Defense* (Brookings Institution Press).

10–12. The final book is actually a trilogy of reports—government reports. In 1998, Congress chartered the U.S. Commission on National Security/Twenty-First Century, also known as the National Security Study Group, to produce three reports that would constitute a comprehensive national security review, available to the administration that would take office in January 2001. Donald Rumsfeld's in-house Pentagon efforts undercut the political significance of these reports, but they were nonetheless prescient and astute. The reports are: *New World Coming*; *Seeking a National Strategy*; and *Road Map for National Security*. They're available at www.nssg.gov.

Web Sites

Among the joys of the twenty-first century is the ability to get real news and serious analysis from a seemingly endless variety of Internet sources. National security affairs are no exception. Even though a great deal of information must remain either classified or proprietary, publicly available web sites can provide the interested citizen with more than ample context and data.

The fundamental site is www.defenselink.mil, the Pentagon's home page. This provides official reports, publications, press releases, and other data. It also offers links, directly and indirectly, to thousands of other military web sites: the Armed Services and unified commands; bases; war colleges; publications. Defenselink also links to Congress and other government agencies. In addition, many of these sites provide extensive bibliographies and reading lists. Another indispensable military site, www.dtic.mil, actually produces many of the publications. As the old recruiting slogan goes, "It's a great place to start."

Many universities maintain active national security programs of various kinds. Columbia University provides a first-rate bibliographical and resource listing. Try www.columbia.edu/cu/libraries/indiv/lehman/guides/isc.html.

Think tanks and research institutes also offer excellent studies and links to other academic and policy sites. Some of these are large, "full service" establishments, addressing many issues; others are single-issue, dealing only in defense. To mention a few of the biggies:

Heritage Foundation, conservative. www.heritage.org.

Center for Strategic and International Studies, moderate right to centrist, www.csis.org.

Brookings Institution, centrist to moderate left, www.brookings.org.

Cato Institute, libertarian, www.cato.org.

RAND Corporation, perhaps the archetype of the modern think tank, founded to support the Air Force and now active in many other fields. www.rand.org.

Some of the more significant all-or-mostly defense establishments:

Center for Strategic and Budgetary Assessments, non-ideological, transformation-oriented, taken seriously within the Beltway. www.csbaonline.org.

Business Executives for National Security, centrist in both directions, influential in many aspects of defense. www.bens.org.

Center for Defense Information, left-liberal, occasionally infuriating. www.cdi.org.

John Pike a former weapons specialist for the Federation of American Scientists, has never met a weapon he liked, but generally knows what he's talking about. His old site, www.fas.org, is still valuable. Pike's new web site, www.nationalsecurity.org, is always worth a look, and usually more.

Lexington Institute, a conservative site filled with folks who never met a weapon they didn't like. www.lexingtoninstitute.org.

A couple specialized sites:

AnSer (Analytic Services) runs an Institute for Homeland Security: www.homelandsecurity.org

Center for Security Policy, run by Frank Gaffney, a former Pentagon official and long-time ballistic missile defense advocate, stays abreast of this field. www.security-policy.org.

Three other web sites favored by Pentagon working types and serious thinkers:

www.belisarius.com

www.companycommand.com

www.d-n-i.net

Finally, you may have noticed that many of the footnotes in the text cite "Early Bird." That's the Pentagon media clipping service known officially as "Current News," produced by the Current News Service of the Armed Forces Information Service, Office of the Assistant Secretary of Defense for Public Affairs, in collaboration with the Defense Technical Information Center. Five days a week, (holidays excluded) three long documents appear. The "Early Bird" proper reproduces the morning's major stories, opinion columns, and editorials. The "Supplement" offers a larger selection from the nation's papers and magazines, and a good sampling of the trade and professional press. "Radio-TV Defense Dialog" does transcripts of selected major radio and TV coverage. In hard copy, these documents can run from a hundred pages on a quiet day to several hundred in time of crisis or war.

Alas, only those with government or military domain addresses or otherwise authorized can access the Early Bird. Copyright restrictions and arrangements with publishers prohibit more general distribution. But if you can access, it's fantastic.

And by the by, don't forget Discovery Institute and www.discovery.org.

Appendix B
General Principles of Transformation

Ever since the RMA got started, people have been coming up with lists of axioms and criteria for military transformation. Most of these get jargonized very quickly, and although it's always gratifying to sling about phrases such as "precision maneuver" and "network-centric warfare" and the rest, the general reader soon succumbs to a condition known as MEGO, or, "Mine Eyes Glaze Over." Therefore, to keep it simple, we offer seven easy maxims, taken from the text and distilled.

Homeland Security Comes First.

The first responsibility of any government is the protection of its citizens, territory, and material values. In the current context, this means creation of a Homeland Defense Command to provide the military components of a Homeland Security Agency, which will be established after the next disaster, or when it becomes apparent that the current Office of Homeland Security possesses neither the budget nor the clout to get everybody organized. Homeland security also requires enhanced air and coastal defense, and defense against limited ballistic missile strikes. As a general rule, whatever can be done by the Army and Air National Guards should be done by them. This may mean re-orienting large sections of the Army Guard away from foreign missions. It may also require creating several new kinds of Guard units and levels of participation.

American Military Forces Are Expeditionary.

With the exception of homeland defense—a vital yet limited task—American forces must be structured to go almost anywhere to do everything from major war to humanitarian relief. Expeditionary forces are always far more expensive than forces that fight in or around home.

American Forces Must Achieve and Maintain Full Spectrum Dominance via Transformation.

This is Pentagonese for the ability to win anywhere, anytime, doing whatever might be needed. An additional requirement: America must be able to conduct RDOs (Rapid Decisive Operations) across this spectrum, whenever possible.

America Is an Aerospace Power—the First and Only in History.

The great American comparative advantage is aerospace. As Desert Storm and the Afghan campaign demonstrated, we're only beginning to explore the possibilities. Air supremacy—we do what we want; they don't do nothin'—must never be lost or even endangered. America must develop a far more aggressive space power policy, doctrine, and force structure, including systems for offensive and defensive warfare in space and, over time, the placement of precision weapons able to attack targets below.

Systems Proliferate but Effects Converge.

This is one of two conceptual keys to transformation. It means simply that there are many ways to accomplish the same missions. As a rule, whatever can be done from the air or space probably should be done from the air or space, and more can be done all the time. Beyond that, American forces should be restructured to take maximum advantage of these synergies. This means getting beyond inter- and intra-service rivalries.

Specialization plus Mobility Yields Versatility.

It's a big planet. Many assets, from generic air power to what are known as HD/LD (High Demand, Low Density) units—interpreters, special intelligence and communications services, etc.—will always be stretched thin. The key is to specialize without tying these assets, as has been done since World War II, to specific locations.

Twenty-First Century Threats and Technologies Empower Eighteenth Century Virtues.

The role of the citizenry must be greatly expanded. Using new training techniques and tools—distance learning, virtual reality simulation, etc.—citizen-soldiers may attain unprecedented levels of pre-mobilization readiness. In many cases, citizen-soldiers bring skills that the military can't afford to generate on its own in sufficient quantity: computer experts, doctors, engineers and scientists, interpreters, to name only a few. Interested citizens should be given more opportunities to serve in military or para-military roles where they can contribute as specialists. In the past, the services have been reluctant to offer more than minimal opportunities in this manner. Specialist officer and warrant officer direct commissioning programs into the National Guard and service reserves should be expanded. In the twenty-first century, the Minuteman tradition will and should take on some novel forms—the part-time cyberwarrior and satellite controller as well as the man with the rifle. But in any case, the Founding Fathers' notion of a citizenry actively involved in the common defense at many levels in many ways is once again germane.

There is also an eighth principle: The American people must understand what transformation is, and why it's so essential, *and let their representatives know it*. When in DC, politicians listen to each other. When they're home, they listen to their constituents. Only a minority of senators and representatives specialize in defense. But all should know that their level of support for the hard work of transformation will be scrutinized. Beltway and Pentagon business-as-usual is no longer either tolerable or safe. And in America, elections come often.

Printed in the United States
3819

9 780963 865465